PRESTON'S MILITARY HERITAGE

Keith Johnson

AMBERLEY

A poignant message on the Penwortham war memorial in 2018.

This book is dedicated to the memory of all whose actions and deeds have created Preston's military heritage, and to those who seek to preserve it.

First published 2019

Amberley Publishing
The Hill, Stroud
Gloucestershire, GL5 4EP

www.amberley-books.com

Copyright © Keith Johnson, 2019

Logo source material courtesy of Gerry van Tonder

The right of Keith Johnson to be identified as the Author of this work has been asserted in accordance with the Copyrights, Designs and Patents Act 1988.

ISBN 978 1 4456 8405 5 (print)
ISBN 978 1 4456 8406 2 (ebook)

British Library Cataloguing in Publication Data.
A catalogue record for this book is available from the British Library.

Origination by Amberley Publishing.
Printed in Great Britain.

Contents

Introduction   5

1. When Romans Roamed the Boundaries   6

2. The Vikings Buried Treasures   11

3. Making Headlines in the Past   15

4. Military Might of Preston   20

5. A Monumental Day on Lune Street   28

6. Crimean Cannons from Sebastopol   31

7. Boer War – From Preston to South Africa   34

8. Patriotic Pride in Preston Pals   38

9. Letters from the Western Front   42

10. The Munition Lasses   45

11. The Fallen Football Heroes   48

12. Streets of Remembrance – Lest We Forget   50

13. Raising a Glass to the Returning Heroes   53

14. Why War?   56

15. The Sacrifice of Our Sailors   58

16. Weapons of War   60

17. Threat from the Sky Above   64

18. Preston Railway Station Memories   67

19. Home for Soldiers Galore – Fulwood Barracks   70

20. Military Treasures Aplenty – Infantry Museum   77

21. War Memorials and Memories   82

22. Remembrance – Part of Our Heritage   90

About the Author   96

Acknowledgements   96

Lest we forget.

Introduction

Tasked with researching the military heritage of Preston, I found myself on an enthralling journey. Preston and the outskirts have been touched by events from around the globe from as early as the conquering Roman years; those days when invading Vikings came our way and when blood was shed for king and country.

Consequently, it was quite a mixture that captured my imagination: Roman roads, buried treasures, bloody confrontations, letters from serving soldiers, captured cannons, the exploits of munition workers, footballers who went to war, the perils of the sea, a railway station with cups of char for free, the threats from the sky above, a military barracks for fighting soldiers, inns and their signs paying tribute to the military, streets named in remembrance of battles and those involved in conflicts, military equipment skilfully constructed, museums and their collections, countless war memorials all painstakingly constructed, and remembrance that it is clearly not restricted to Remembrance Sunday – all being worthy of mention.

Many generations of Preston families have been touched by the consequences of conflicts and confrontations, both at home and abroad. There have been countless heroic acts by those who proudly displayed the pride of Preston in their deeds, their courage and resolve quite amazing. And those left behind at home enduring worry and anguish before their loved one returned, while others were left bereft by tragic news.

Fortunately, the people of the city of Preston have preserved and protected that military heritage and there are numerous reminders of those engaged in military service down the centuries. Our museums have ensured that those who served are remembered with deep gratitude, with displays, attractions and exhibitions commonplace – none more so than the Lancashire Infantry Museum within the Fulwood Barracks where a lavish collection of military treasures are stored along with records of those who served.

Preston's military pride was highlighted once again in 2018, at the time of the centenary of the Armistice, when an impressive parade made its way to the cenotaph to pay tribute to the fallen.

My research enabled me to shed some light on our military past and I became aware of the mighty military heritage within the streets, churches, museums and graveyards of Preston and beyond the boundaries – 'lest we forget'. It is clear Preston displays a great gratitude to all those who served and willingly fought for the freedom cherished by us all.

In conclusion, Preston is a place where you could linger awhile and soak up plenty of military heritage, where the memories of those who served is preserved for future generations.

1. When Romans Roamed the Boundaries

Unfortunately, it would be simply untrue to say the Romans left Preston a great legacy of military heritage. In truth we have to look to the outskirts of the city to find any significant evidence of the Roman invasion of Britain and a visit to the Ribchester Roman Museum, opened in 1915, reveals all on the matter.

At the time of the Roman invasion of Britain, Preston was, in many ways, of little significance, although the surrounding area was of interest to the invaders. The conquest of Britain took place gradually, beginning in AD 43 under the Emperor Claudius and being complete over forty years later. The north was only conquered around AD 75, when it was populated by a people the Romans described as 'warlike Brigantes' who lived in tribes.

When Charles Hardwick wrote his *History of the Borough of Preston* in 1857, he remarked that publication had been delayed partly because he had recently learnt of the discovery of a Roman station at Walton-le-Dale; that excavations at Castle Hill, Penwortham, had unearthed interesting remains; and that the discovery of the Cuerdale Hoard revealed more secrets.

In 1840, the remains of a Roman fortified camp were found at Walton-le-Dale, axes and other ancient weapons in abundance, when they laid the foundations for a cotton factory at Walton Flats, close to the River Ribble. In 1870, the remains of a Roman road were uncovered, and further Roman road remains have been traced in Fulwood, Cadley, Broughton and Barton. The road from Kirkham to Ribchester passed through Fulwood in the days when trees flourished in the forest land, following the route of Watling Street Road. At some point this Roman road was intersected by the road from Lancaster to Walton-le-Dale. The present-day Cadley Causeway and Watling Street Road bear witness that Romans legions marched this way. Indeed, some former residents of Fulwood Barracks with lively imaginations have spoken of seeing, on dark, stormy nights, a glimpse of the ghostly image of a group of Roman soldiers making their way along the parade ground, which is said to be the original path of the road before the barracks were built.

The odd coin or two have been unearthed in both Ribbleton and Ashton too – a further indicator of Roman activity. A couple of coins of Emperor Nerva dating from AD 96–98 and Emperor Licinius from AD 307–324 were found in Ribbleton, and a coin of Emperor Gailienus from AD 260–268 was discovered in Haslam Park and they are exhibited in the Harris Museum.

Ribchester, of course, is noted for its Roman remains and has a splendid museum dedicated to the days of the mighty Roman Empire. The fort at Ribchester was known as Bremetennacum and is thought to have been founded by the Romans around AD 78, when Agricola conquered this part of the country.

The Romans, pushing up towards Scotland under Agricola, ever alert to utilise the military advantages of the contour of the land, saw in Penwortham an important point

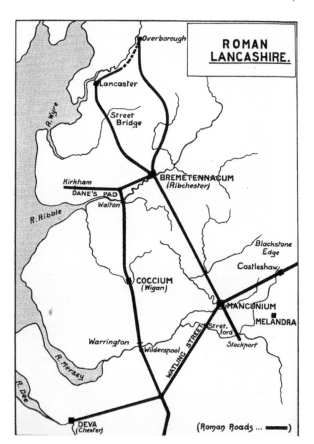

Right: Roman roads have been traced throughout Lancashire.

Below: The River Ribble at Ribchester was essential for supplies.

of their northward line of march. Castle Hill, it is credibly surmised, was thus fortified to guard the ford of the Ribble and provide a general vantage point on the road through the north-west. Although later there would be a Saxon/Norman castle there, built *c.* 1071, it is thought that the site was originally a military depot of some importance during the Roman occupation. Hardwick, when he examined the Castle Hill site, unearthed the remains of a Norman motte-and-bailey castle. He discovered a mound of earth 30 feet high by 25 feet wide, the motte, with a courtyard area, the bailey, at its base with buildings and stables. He believed that the castle and keep would have been on top of the mound of earth. The whole site was surrounded by timber defences.

The Ribchester Museum gives you the opportunity to imagine the men who ruled this country with an iron hand for 400 years. Therein lie many of the relics unearthed in Ribchester during the intervening years; relics of a powerful race that played a significant role in the history of our nation. Among the wonders you will see is the replica of a helmet worn by a Roman soldier on ceremonial occasions. It was found by a Ribchester schoolboy, the son of a clog maker, in 1796 while playing on waste ground behind their cottage. According to a newspaper report of 1798, the young lad had been sliding down a bank when part of the earth gave way and the find was discovered. It is a magnificently ornate bronze helmet, comprising a hinged visor and a domed headpiece. The subsequently named 'Ribchester Helmet' became part of small hoard of metal items, believed to have belonged to a Roman soldier from around AD 120. The original helmet has been in the British Museum since 1814. A gold Roman coin discovered in January 1835 by John Scarsbrick as he strolled along the banks of the Ribble, around 150 yards from

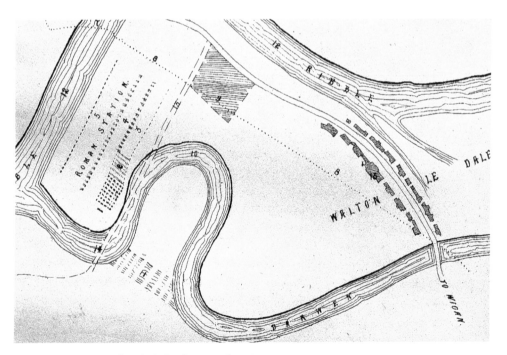

The Roman site at Walton-le-Dale, discovered in 1840.

The Castle Hill site at Penwortham was a strategic location for Romans.

Ribchester Church, added to the fascination. On one side was a figure of the 'Goddess Faustina', and it was believed to be from around AD 150. In 1876, the tombstone of an Asturian cavalryman was discovered by chance on the riverbank close to the museum. The gravestone was carved from local stone and shows a cavalryman riding down a Celtic warrior, showing no mercy as he impales the barbarian foe with his spear.

The fort was the base for a garrison of cavalry troops who patrolled the area and controlled the local dwellers. Numerous excavations have discovered that rectangular wooden buildings used as workshops and dwellings existed. The civilian site, beyond the fort boundaries, was more or less the size of the village of Ribchester today. Craftsmen such as blacksmiths and saddlers would have been at work here, producing essential goods for civilian and military needs.

The settlement was also the site of the Roman baths, a substantial brick-built construction. A couple of Roman temples also existed within the boundaries. Excavations in 1908 uncovered the remains of the granaries, where essential supplies were stored for the garrison, the pillars having supported a flagged floor. Research suggests that the fort at Ribchester was occupied into the fourth century, although archaeological evidence points to little activity in the vicus or neighbourhood after the second century.

It is believed that when the Romans departed from Britain to defend their own country, the local tribesmen broke into the fortress and plundered the premises, setting fire to stores and structures, including a couple of granaries.

As recently as the 1980s and 1990s, excavations by the Oxford Archaeology North organisation at Walton-le Dale, now the site of the Capitol Centre, have confirmed the belief that the site was involved chiefly in trade and manufacturing of military equipment for the Roman forces. In January 2019, archaeologists from Salford University unearthed a further section of Roman road at Cuerdale, along with some pottery on the site of a new retail park development.

In conclusion, research has shown that the Romans did indeed build a network of roads and forts along the valley of Belisama Fluvis (the River Ribble), that north of the river there were forts at Kirkham and Ribchester, and that the River Ribble was a crucial factor for both transport and trade. It is clear that the Romans were very much part of our military heritage. Perhaps, like me, when you travel along Watling Street Road you might give a thought to the fact that Romans once roamed that way too.

A replica of the Roman helmet is on display in the Harris Museum.

The Ribchester Roman Museum takes you back to Roman days.

2. The Vikings Buried Treasures

The treasures that became known as the Cuerdale Hoard were discovered on an evening in mid-May 1840 by workmen who were repairing the south embankment of the River Ribble at Cuerdale. Preston folk are well aware that Preston, once the capital of Amounderness, dating back to at least AD 934 when it was given to the Archbishop of York by King Aethelstan, was once the haunt of Vikings and Saxons. A written description of the region was given to King Aethelstan at that time, confirming its important geographical position due to its river and access to the sea and stating thus, 'From the sea along the Cocker to the source of that river, from that source straight to another spring which is called in Saxon, Dunshop, thus down to the river let to the Hodder, in the same direction to the Ribble and thus along that river through the middle of the channel to the sea.'

Thomas Southworth is credited with being one of the fourteen men who found the Cuerdale Hoard and it is reported that at least five of them were given a coin. It was the greatest silver Viking treasure ever found in Britain or in Europe. It comprised over 8,500 items, with around 7,500 coins and 1,000 silver objects, including ingots, amulets, rings, brooches and armlets. The hoard was inside what remained of a lead-lined chest.

It is usual when the coroner's court sits that a death has occurred and the inquest jury have to consider the circumstance; however, in mid-August 1840 that was not the case, as Coroner John Hargreaves conducted an inquisition at Preston's Bull Inn. The court was conducted under the provisions of a statute of Henry I, which directed that when any treasure was found the coroner shall summon a jury to inquire into the circumstances of the find, and ascertain whether the treasure belongs to the Crown.

The court heard that in mid-May 1840 great excitement had been created when a number of workmen employed to repair the embankment of the River Ribble at Cuerdale had, during their operations, uncovered a buried treasure. It was contained in a lead chest, which had become so decayed and corroded that it broke asunder in their attempts to extract it from the ground and the enclosed valuables began to pour out. The workmen, overjoyed at their discovery, cried out with delight and their excitement was overheard by the keeper of the nearby Cuerdale Hall, who hurried to see what the commotion was. The men were on their knees around the treasure and in the midst of a general scramble to pocket the untold riches. The keeper, however, soon made them understand they must leave the treasure untouched. Consequently, although the odd coin had been plundered, the treasure was forthwith collected and by late evening was deposited in the bank of Messrs Pedder & Fleetwood.

To everyone's astonishment it was reckoned the treasure consisted of up to 8,000 coins from the reigns of Ethelred, Alfred and Edward the Elder, along with large ingots of silver, bracelets, bridle bits and rings, making up to 1,000 items altogether. It was thought the treasure had been buried up to a thousand years earlier due to some of the Anglo-Saxon coins having dates from AD 855.

Above: Part of the Cuerdale Hoard, which caused great excitement.

Left: A stone marker was placed on the site of the discovery.

The land where the treasure trove had been discovered belonged to William Assheton of Downham Hall, near Clitheroe, and his claim to the bounty saw him represented by John Addison, while the solicitor general represented Queen Victoria. It was stated that the total weight of silver was 1,265 ounces, with a market value of £285 – the equivalent of £28,000 in today's money according to the Bank of England inflation calculations, although in reality the ornamental value of many of the silver items and their antiquarian market value made the trove many times more valuable.

The attorney general contended that the find was a treasure trove and, as it was bullion found in the ground, the owner unknown, they belonged to the Crown. Mr Addison claimed that there was no evidence that the haul had been buried and that it could have been abandoned; the chest could possibly even have been washed ashore and covered with sand down the centuries. As such, he argued, the Crown had no claim to the property, which rightly belonged to the lord of the manor, Mr Assheton.

After a long and able summing up, the jury retired to consider their verdict. After around fifteen minutes the jury returned and the foreman delivered the following decision: 'We find the articles are the property of Her Majesty in right of her Duchy of Lancaster, as treasure trove.'

It was expected that, as the attorney general had promised earlier, the treasure would be distributed among the public collections in the county. What became known as the Cuerdale Hoard, the greatest silver Viking treasure ever found in Britain, was indeed distributed between museums and collectors by the Duchy of Lancaster – over 170 institutions and individuals the recipients. The Harris Museum in Preston is the present keeper of eighty-eight coins that were originally given to the Preston Institute. It is believed the treasure was buried around AD 905 as the Vikings originally only used solid silver for trade – like the ingots and hacksilver found. Anglo-Saxon, Scandinavian and Arabic coins were also among the haul.

In more recent times, one theory suggested the treasure might have belonged to forces who were plotting a campaign in Ireland and who assembled in the Ribble Valley after being vanquished from Dublin, albeit temporarily, in AD 902. A considerable amount of the bullion has been identified as of Irish origin, and upwards of forty brooches appear to have Irish connections.

Further evidence of those Viking days came in 1822 when a Viking burial was found near Claughton Hall, north of Preston. A wooden structure was found inside a mound with iron weapons, jewellery and a stone axe head, all thought to be from 2,000 BC. It is believed the Vikings may well have used a Bronze Age burial mound. A pair of oval brooches were discovered from that Claughton burial, the kind Viking women wore on each shoulder to secure their clothing. They are believed to be from around AD 850–950, and they were found bound together in cloth with two beads and a molar tooth. All these specimens are on view in the Harris Museum, and Lancashire folk view the Curedale Hoard as part of the military heritage left by those Viking invaders.

In July 2018, the people of Preston had a glimpse of what those Viking days were like when a re-enactment society set up a Viking encampment on the Preston Market Square, displaying crafts, cooking habits and formidable weapons.

The visiting 'Vikings' set up camp on the Preston Market Square in July 2018.

Ready for battle – the modern Viking warriors.

3. Making Headlines in the Past

In the days before newspapers became an essential chronicle of news, many significant events took place that were worthy of hitting the headlines. Although it was only in 1886 that the *Lancashire Evening Post* hit the newspaper stands, the former *LEP* historian Terry Farrell, in one of the paper's anniversary issues, speculated on what the newspaper would have reported as they rushed to meet the daily deadline. Using his inspiration, what follows are a selection of headline news features that reflect Preston's military heritage and could have been reported by the scribes of today, had they been transported back in time.

First Edition, 1 May 1328
Peace Treaty Confirmed for Scottish Chieftain Who Plundered Preston
Today in Northampton, the Treaty of Edinburgh, signed by Robert the Bruce, was ratified by the English Parliament. The agreement between England and Scotland recognises Scotland as an independent nation and Robert the Bruce as its king. For over twenty years, first Edward I and then his son Edward II have been fighting wars against the Scots, notably the Battle of Bannockburn in 1314, in which Bruce defeated the army of Edward II.

Back in 1306, Edward I halted in Preston on his way to join battle with the Scots, issuing a proclamation urging local men to join his forces with many volunteers joining his ranks. It was a tactic later used by Edward II, who was also successful in recruiting local men to take up arms for king and country. Still fresh in our memories are the Scots many successful incursions into the northern counties. One of the most destructive of those being in 1323 when Robert the Bruce entered into England by Carlisle, then kept on his pillaging through Cumberland, Westmorland and Lancaster to Preston. After burning the town, the Scots crossed the River Ribble by the ford at Red Scar and destroyed the lower hall at Samlesbury. Looting the chalice, missal and vestments from Samlesbury Church as they went on their rampaging way to Hoghton, where cattle, lances and saddles were seized. It is hoped the treaty will bring to an end the fierce fighting that has gone on for many years.

First Edition, 18 August 1617
King James Had a Knight to Remember
On his way back from Scotland last week, James I visited Lancaster and then went on to Hornby Castle before visiting the Tyldesleys at Myerscough Lodge, near Garstang, where he hunted and feasted. Over the weekend the king and his courtiers were guests of Sir Richard Hoghton at Hoghton Tower. Last night a magnificent banquet was laid on in the monarch's honour, attended by many wealthy families of the county. According to a

Hoghton Tower, where James I dined and had a 'knight' to remember.

witness of the event, King James was in jovial spirits and enjoyed the main course of loin beef so much that he claimed it was worthy of a knighthood. He asked for a sword, laid it upon the beef and declared it to be known in future as 'Sir Loin'. After staying overnight, the king and his entourage moved on to Lathom House, the seat of the Stanleys, where he will remain two days before continuing his journey south. During his stay he is expected to knight half a dozen gentlemen, including John Talbot from Preston.

First Edition, 10 February 1643
Adam Morte and Son Killed by Cromwell's Troops
As fierce fighting continues in the town news comes through that Adam Morte, who was elected mayor in 1642 but declined to take the office and was consequently fined 100 marks, was killed along with his son as the Parliamentarians stormed Preston. Having chosen to defend the town with the Royalist troops, both father and son fought bravely together before being slain. The pair fought shoulder to shoulder in defence of the parish church, which had been commandeered by the Royalists as their garrison. The Parliamentary forces, led by Sir John Seaton, were too strong for the brave Royalists who, despite building fortifications, were overwhelmed and it is feared many have been killed or taken prisoner.

Only last year Adam Morte had been recognised as one of the most ardent supporters of the Royalist cause as Lord Derby recruited volunteers for the king's forces. Funds of over £8,700 were raised in Lancashire to enable a military force of 400 horse soldiers and 2,000 infantry to be assembled, with Morte the custodian of the cash. Late news: it is believed that Captain Hoghton, the brother of Sir Gilbert Hoghton of Hoghton Tower, is among those slain.

First Edition, 17 August 1648
The Last Stand

Preston became the scene of one of the bloodiest battles in Britain's history today as Royalists and Roundhead forces fought each other ferociously in and around the town. General Oliver Cromwell led his army of 6,000 Parliamentary troops from Yorkshire to

> **Preston, August 17, 1648**
>
> Gentlemen,
>
> It hath pleased God this day to show His great power by making the army successful against the common enemy.
>
> We lay last night at Mr Sherbourne's of Stony-hurst, nine miles from Preston, which was within three miles of the Scottish quarters. We advanced betimes next morning towards Preston with a desire to engage the enemy, and by that time our For-lorn (infantry) had engaged the enemy. We were about four miles from Preston and thereupon we advanced the whole army and the enemy being drawn out upon a moor (Ribbleton) betwixt us and the town, the armies of both sides engaged.
>
> After a sharp bout, continuing for three of four hours, it pleased God to enable us to give the enemy a defeat which I hope we shall improve by God's assistance to their utter ruin . . . We can assure you we have many prisoners and many of those of quality and many slain. The principal whereof with Duke Hamilton is on the south side of Ribble and Darwen bridge and we lying with the greatest part of our army close to them . . . It will be our care that they shall not passover any ford beneath the bridge to go northwards nor to come over betwixt us and Whalley . . .
>
> That is all at present from
> Your very humble servant
>
> **Oliver Cromwell**

Oliver Cromwell praised his troops.

Stoneyhurst and confronted the English Royalists, under Sir Marmaduke Langdale, at their Ribbleton Moor camp, near Eaves Brook, scattering them into the country lanes.

Langdale, with the remnants of his beleaguered Royalist troops, struggled bravely back into town. There they met up with some of the Duke of Hamilton's Scottish soldiers, who had come down from the north to oppose Cromwell and restore their beloved Charles I to the throne.

Fierce fighting took place in Church Street and the Duke of Hamilton and some of his men retreated into Fishergate and down to the ford at Penwortham. As they fled, they swam across the river to meet the southern contingent of his troops fleeing on Walton Summit.

Meanwhile, Cromwell and his men continued to force the rest of the Royalists and Scottish troops from Church Street into the Avenham area and down to the bridge over the River Ribble. On and around the bridge, the Royalists made a brave stand as hand to hand fighting took place with swords, pikes and muskets. However, faced with the might of Cromwell's forces they continued to fall back and were forced to flee over the bridge that spans the River Darwen.

By nightfall many Royalist and Scottish troops had been slain, wounded or taken prisoner, with the rest fleeing bloodied and beaten into the darkness of the night.

Reports earlier in the day indicate that some of the Scottish troops have fled into the Fylde, while others went north, pursued by Parliamentary troops, who killed a number of them. General Cromwell resumed the chase this morning as the Royalists retreated through Chorley to the south.

First Edition, 12 November 1715
Rebels Surrender – Over 200 Royalists Slain
Fierce fighting in Preston between Jacobite rebels and the forces of George I ended today, with the surrender of the entire rebel force. The Jacobites had set out from Scotland and were intent on reaching London to overthrow the king in order that the son of the former James II would replace him on the throne.

On arriving in Preston just two days ago, the rebels, who numbered around 1,600 men, proclaimed James II's son as James III of England from the steps of the market cross. Local people cheered in support of them, showing their apparent dislike of King George, who they viewed as a Hanoverian usurper.

Fighting occurred in the centre of town and barricades were placed at the four main entrances. As the rebels tried to win control of the bridge over the River Ribble at Walton-le-Dale, the Royalist army, under the command of General Wills, forced them to withdraw.

Overnight, General Carpenter, another Royalist commander, arrived from Clitheroe, having been summoned by Sir Henry Hoghton, of Hoghton Tower. Carpenter's superior forces soon forced the rebels to surrender, with the document of surrender being signed in the Mitre Inn on the eastern side of the marketplace.

The bulk of the rebel prisoners are imprisoned in the Preston Parish Church, where sympathetic townsfolk are supplying them with food and blankets as the weather has turned bitterly cold. It is reckoned that at least 217 Royalists were killed during the bloody

Time to surrender for the rebels in November 1715.

conflict, while the defeated Jacobite rebels reported that seventeen of their forces had been killed and over twenty injured severely.

First reports from the Royalist camp suggest that the leaders of the Jacobite rebels were likely to be put on trial for high treason.

Footnote: Detailed accounts of the Preston battles during the Civil War and the Jacobite Rebellion can be found in *Secret Preston* by Keith Johnson (Amberley Publishing, 2015).

4. Military Might of Preston

During his conflicts with James IV of Scotland, Henry VIII reportedly recruited Lancashire men, including some from Preston as it had one of the larger populations of the county. It is recorded that in 1553, Amounderness, of which Preston was the capital, supplied 300 men under a levy by Queen Mary. The raising of the militia was entrusted to the lord lieutenants of the counties under an Act passed in 1558. A year later, Amounderness raised a force of over 200 armoured men and 360 unarmoured troops towards the national defences. The Spanish Armada alert and the Parliamentary conflict surrounding Charles I led to meetings and intentions to raise substantial forces as influential county gentlemen met at Preston to formulate plans, although nothing significant was enacted.

When we consider the infantrymen, Preston's closest and longest relationship has been with the Loyal Regiment (North Lancashire), whose oldest antecedent, the 47th Regiment of Foot, was raised in 1741 and earned early distinction in Canada and America at the Battle of Quebec in 1759 and Bunker's Hill in 1775.

Prior to 1751 regiments were known by the name of their colonel, their title changing with each new leader. They then became known by consecutive numbers, which roughly followed their order of raising. Only in 1782 was it thought proper to encourage local recruitment for the infantry by including county names in the titles. Thus, the 47th Regiment of Foot, who already recruited in Lancashire, were granted the additional title of the Lancashire Regiment.

In 1797, the 3rd Royal Lancashire Militia Regiment was formed of volunteers, with its headquarters in Preston. The same year saw a corps established named the Royal Preston Volunteers, commanded by Lieutenant-Colonel Nicholas Grimshaw, the future guild mayor, and Lieutenant-Colonel John Watson, the pioneering cotton factory owner. These troops camped upon the ground to the rear of where the Fulwood Barracks would be built. The great bulk of the volunteers at this time were working men and, as working hours were very long, they had to use Sunday for training purposes. They often cleaned their muskets in the forenoon, were drilled in the Market Square in the afternoon and, when daylight permitted, marched down to the Marsh for exercise.

As long ago as the Napoleonic Wars (1803–15), the 3rd Royal Lancashire Militia were embodied to take part in the defence of the country on the prospect of invasion by the French. They journeyed to many parts of the country, garrisoning Portsmouth, Plymouth, Gosport, Dover and other strategic locations.

In January 1809, after the great drain upon English military resources following the Continental wars, there was a meeting at Preston's Bull Inn of the deputy lieutenants of Lancashire following a demand from the country. That summer, Preston alone, under Lieutenant-Colonel Grimshaw, mustered over 1,000 rank and file troops for a month's training to be ready for duty.

The 47th Regiment were not involved in the first half of the long wars with revolutionary France, but from 1809 they provided garrisons at Gibraltar, Tarif and Cadiz. Within two years they were playing their part in the hard-fought victory of Barrosa and they later marched forward to join Wellington's army, fighting a heavy rearguard action at Puente Largo in late October 1812. They later played a prominent part in the decisive Battle of Vitoria, the storming of San Sebastian, where they suffered heavy casualties, and were among the first British troops to enter France before being heavily engaged at the Battle of Nave.

The 47th Regiment became used to service abroad in the outposts of the empire as from 1782 they spent only four years out of seventy in England. The regiment generally served in overseas garrisons, guarding British trade routes and the frontiers of the rapidly expanding colonial empire. Among their operations were the capture of Montevideo in 1807, two expeditions against pirates in the Persian Gulf, the Mahratta War and the Burmese War of 1825–26.

By 1854, when the Crimean War broke out, the militia regiments, including the 3rd Royal Lancashire, were called up. They went out to Gibraltar in June 1855 under the command of Colonel Wilson Patten and served there for twelve months. At Gibraltar the regiment was around 1,000 strong and did duty there in place of regular soldiers, who were despatched to the seat of war in the Crimea. On their return from relief duties they were quartered at Preston.

The 47th Regiment formed part of an Anglo-French expedition sent in 1854 to capture the Russian Baltic Sea naval base of Sebastopol on the Crimean peninsula. Their major actions were at the Alma, the Battle of Inkerman, and the capture of Sebastopol. The 47th Regiment suffered over 400 battle casualties, including eighty-two dead, and even heavier losses from disease and sickness.

Franco-British relationships had a roller coaster ride from the close partnership of the Crimean War to downright hostility, including the threat of a French invasion that roused the whole country in 1859. With this threat in mind, men from operatives to merchants were keen to rush to arms for the defence of the country. At the end of May 1859, William Birley, the Mayor of Preston, arranged a meeting with regards to the volunteer question in the Town Hall. Consequently, it was decided to establish a volunteer rifle corps for the borough of Preston, and the neighbourhood and the corps was given the title of the 11th Lancashire.

The first enrolment took place in October and the first drill was undertaken weeks later in the old Corn Exchange. In need of extra funds, they raided the coffers of the old militia, which had ceased duty in 1815, and leading businesses in the town contributed generously.

The HQ of the Preston Rifle Volunteers were originally in Fox Street and later on their depot moved to Lord Street, with the drill ground being the open land on Lancaster Road, next to the Earl Street police station where the Municipal Buildings now stand.

It became common practice for the 3rd Royal Lancashire Militia to assemble for a twenty-seven-day training session each summer, as they did in early July 1876 when the troops mustered at the Militia Barracks on New Hall Lane. On that occasion over 600 men and officers marched from their HQ on Stanley Street, built in 1854, to the Preston railway station to catch a train to Southport, where they would live under canvas for the duration of the term of exercise and military manoeuvres.

NOTICE

IS HEREBY GIVEN YOU,

THAT you (being enrolled to serve in the AMOUNDERNESS REGIMENT of LOCAL MILITIA,) are to be and appear at *Preston*, in the County of *Lancaster*, on *Tuesday* the *eighth* Day of *June* next, at 9 o'Clock in the Forenoon, then and there to hold yourself in every respect ready to be trained and exercised for the space of 14 Days for the present Year, exclusive of the Days of arriving at and departure from, and marching to and from the Place of Assembly, and you are to behave as the Laws of your Country in general, and those of the Local Militia in particular direct.

And you are hereby required to take Notice, that in case you neglect to appear at the Time and Place aforesaid, you will be deemed a Deserter, and punished as such. Given under my Hand the Nineteenth Day of May 1813.

Left: Militia men recruiting notice of 1813.

Below: Inspection of the Loyal North Lancashire Regiment in 1893, when the 2nd Battalion was based in Mullingar, Ireland. The Glengarry cap worn by some of the men was abolished that year on the introduction of the Field Service cap worn to the present day.

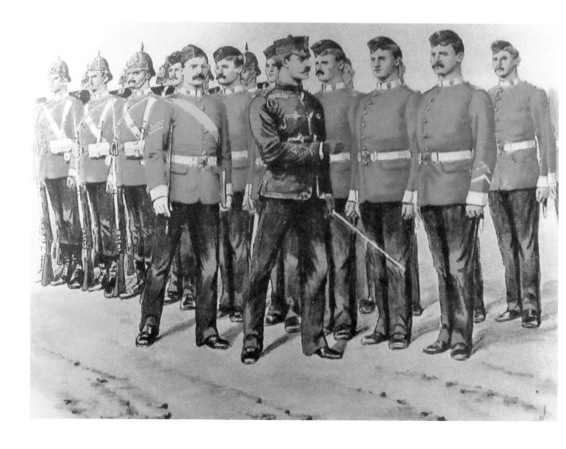

In July 1881, what was known as the Cardwell Reforms took place where the numbered regiments of regular infantry were paired and renamed as battalions of county regiments, with depots in their recruiting areas. In recognition of demographic changes, no less than nine other numbered regiments were allocated to Lancashire, and the 47th Lancashire Regiment became the 1st Battalion. The Loyal North Lancashire Regiment had a depot in the heart of its recruiting area in Preston, with the former 81st Loyal Lincoln Volunteers forming the 2nd Battalion of the regiment. This led to the militia being designated as the 3rd and 4th Battalions of the Loyal North Lancashire Regiment, with assembly for annual training being obligatory.

At the outbreak of the Boer War, the 3rd Battalion of the Loyal North Lancashire Regiment were among the first regiments to offer their service abroad. They were dispatched to Malta in 1899 and within a few more months they requested transfer to the seat of war and saw active service in South Africa before being welcomed home in March 1902, having suffered two losses on the battlefields. Indeed, the South Africa war of 1899–1902 was to see the Loyal North Lancashire Regiment play a significant part in the defence of Kimberley.

Preston men served in all fourteen battalions of the Loyal North Lancashire Regiment that saw active service during the First World War, from 1914–18. The 1st Battalion fought on the Western Front from Mons to the Armistice, earning undying fame as one of the Old Contemptibles battalions of 1914. The 2nd Battalion fought in East Africa and the Middle East before taking part in the final advance on the Western Front. The regular battalions were joined from 1915 onwards by the territorial battalions, and by wartime only service battalions of the regiment, which served in France and Flanders, Gallipoli, Macedonia, Egypt, Palestine and Mesopotamia. The regiment was awarded seventy-five battle honours and three Victoria Crosses, but at a terrible cost: 357 officers and 7,232 other ranks laid down their lives, of whom 1,551 were members of the 1st Battalion.

In 1921, the regimental title was changed to the Loyal Regiment (North Lancashire). Between the wars, after occupation duties in Germany, the cadres of the 1st and 2nd Battalions returned to Fulwood before reforming elsewhere in England. Over the next twenty years they served again worldwide – in Germany, Ireland, Malta, Turkey, China, India, Palestine and Singapore – with security and peacekeeping roles.

When the threat of the Second World War loomed, the 4th Loyals, along with other territorial units, were given duties that transformed them into anti-aircraft defence regiments. Indeed, the 4th Loyal had become known as the 62nd Searchlight Regiment by 1938. They later became the 150th (Loyal) Light Anti-Aircraft Regiment until the end of hostilities.

During the Second World War, the 1st Battalion served in France and Belgium until Dunkirk, where they held the final perimeter at Bergues. In 1943, the 1st Battalion landed in North Africa and fought their way through to Tunis, then took part in the Italian campaign, playing a crucial role in the defence of the Anzio Beachhead. In 1941, the 2nd Loyals fought several rearguard actions against the Japanese in Malaya and Singapore, but then were unfortunately involved in the capitulation of Singapore, spending the next four years in captivity in Korea and elsewhere. The 2nd Battalion was reconstituted in 1942, being renamed the 10th Battalion and leading to active service in Italy. Other battalions

Officers, 3rd Battalion Loyal North Lancashire Regiment.

Above: Officers gather for a photoshoot at Fulwood Barracks in 1897.

Left: Recruiting for the Loyals, an ongoing task.

The 4th Loyal Preston Territorials, August 1914.

Preparing for war at Fulwood Barracks in 1939.

of the Loyals were converted to Royal Armoured Corps or Royal Artillery, fighting in north-west Europe and in Burma. Over the course of the war the regiment earned one Victoria Cross and twenty-one battle honours. Forty-nine officers and 1,050 other ranks of the Loyals lost their lives.

In the immediate aftermath of the Second World War the two regular battalions of the Loyals carried out internal security and occupation duties in Italy, Austria, Egypt, Palestine, Lebanon, Syria, Eritrea and Somaliland. In 1949, the 1st and 2nd Battalions were amalgamated, but operational commitments continued in the Suez Canal zone, at Aqaba in Jordan, and in Trieste. In 1958–59 the Loyals took part in the final stages of the successful counter-insurgency campaign in Malaya. They also served at Wuppertal in Germany in 1960–62 with the British Army on the Rhine. In 1963, they were stationed in Swaziland, and from Malta they were deployed in Aden in 1966 and Libya in 1967.

For the first time ever, in June 1964 the Loyals had the honour of taking over the Queen's Guard. They swapped the parade ground for Buckingham Palace, with 280 men billeted at Chelsea Barracks, ready to march down the Mall in company with the Grenadier Guards they were temporarily relieving. As for the territorials, the local military expanded their facilities with the newly built Kimberley Barracks on Deepdale Road. From 1956 the Royal Artillery, Royal Engineers and the Infantry were operating from there.

No doubt down the centuries various volunteer regiments and corps of the militia have amalgamated and given service not only to Preston but the whole of Lancashire. In October 1967, the regimental colours of the 4th Battalion – the territorials – were laid to rest in the Regimental Chapel of the Preston Parish Church, joining other standards famous in the regiment's history – the most ancient being the tattered remnants of the colours carried by the 47th Regiment of Foot through the shot and shell of the Crimean War.

In late March 1970, at Dover, the Loyal Regiment (North Lancashire) amalgamated with the Lancashire Regiment (Prince of Wales Volunteers) to form the Queen's Lancashire Regiment.

Within six weeks the 1st Battalion was on active service in Northern Ireland, the first of ten operational tours in the troubled province between 1970 and 2003.

In 1982, the battalion, having trained the units sent to recapture the Falkland Islands, were prepared for deployment themselves, but in the event only one company was required. They later supplied reinforcement infantry companies for the Falklands in 2004–05.

In 1996, the battalion carried out peacekeeping missions in Bosnia, and in 2003 they deployed to Basra in the immediate aftermath of the toppling of Saddam Hussein, helping to bring peace and stability to the city. The Queen's Lancashire Regiment were also stationed in Cyprus in 1978–80, 1983 and 2004–05.

For some forty years up to the collapse of the Warsaw Pact the main effort of the British Army was directed towards the North German Plain, where BAOR stood prepared as a vital part of the NATO alliance to resist a Soviet Russian invasion of Western Europe. To set the seal on the Cold War, the regiment had the honour of being the last British

The Queen's Lancashire Regiment on exercise in Cyprus, c. 1980.

The 2nd Battalion on patrol in Afghanistan in 2013.

HM the Queen presents colours to the Duke of Lancaster's Regiment, Fulwood, 26 June 2008.

battalion in Berlin (1992–94), and in 2005–06 they completed their last tour, on that occasion in Osnabruck in the reunited Germany.

At the beginning of July 2006 the 1st Battalion of the Queen's Lancashire Regiment merged with the King's Own Royal Border and the King's Regiment and became the 1st Battalion of the Duke of Lancaster's Regiment. Since then the new regiment, with its headquarters at Preston, has carried out operational tours in Iraq and Afghanistan, earning a high reputation and keeping up the great traditions of all its regimental forebears. In recognition of the Duke of Lancaster's Regiment and the links to Preston's military past, the regiment was granted the freedom of the city of Preston in a ceremony held on the Market Square in July 2007.

I am indebted to the Lancashire Infantry Museum at Fulwood Barracks, from where, during a couple of fascinating visits, I gleaned much of the information required for this chronological look at the history of local infantrymen.

5. A Monumental Day on Lune Street

For so many years the military heritage of Preston was interwoven with the cotton industry of the town. Outside the old Corn Exchange, later Public Hall and currently a public house named simply 1842, is a statue that reflects the events of Saturday, 13 August 1842. It is probably the date most readily recalled by those who study the history of Preston. It was on that day a disturbance took place in Lune Street that left the town in a state of anger and shock. The inhabitants of Preston witnessed a scene of slaughter not seen since the Civil War, as soldiers of the queen came into conflict with the people.

On the third Tuesday of August 1842, inquests were held in the courthouse before coroner Richard Palmer following the deaths of George Sowerbutts, aged nineteen, and Bernard MacNamara, aged seventeen, on the previous Saturday in Lune Street.

The first inquest was relative to the death of George Sowerbutts and it was explained that the introduction of machinery that practically did away with handloom weaving and constant reduction in wages had made many a cotton worker fearful for their future. Consequently, the so-called Chartist Riots had been taking place all over Lancashire, and that week Preston had become the focus of attention, with operatives from nearby towns having paraded the streets in a defiant attitude.

Witnesses testified that on the previous day an unruly mob had visited various factories and, displaying violent behaviour, had forced the workers to turn out. Among those called to testify was Captain Woodford, chief constable of the county police force, who stated that on Saturday before 8 a.m. he went to the Bull Inn where he met Mayor Samuel Horrocks Jr, along with other magistrates and a military detachment of the 72nd

The scene outside the Corn Exchange after the Riot Act was read as the military fired upon the protestors.

Highlanders. He explained how they had confronted the mob on Fishergate and that the military and a body of constables instructed the rioters to disperse.

According to him, some of the mob began throwing stones as they were guided down Lune Street, and when the military and police got close to the Corn Exchange they were furiously pelted with missiles. The mayor was then struck upon the hand with a stone as he proceeded to read the Riot Act. Four or five minutes then elapsed during which the troops were under a shower of missiles, and after this the mayor gave the order to fire as the troops faced the mob near the Corn Exchange. Twenty shots in all were fired, not in a volley but by single firing, and he saw several people fall, particularly one rioter who stood in the middle of the street in the act of hurling a stone. The firing had stopped the mob in their tracks and they began to disperse.

Surgeon Thomas Dixon testified that he had attended to Sowerbutts, who had been hit in the chest with a musket ball, which had broken three of his ribs as it passed through his body. In an insensible state and having lost a lot of blood, he had died on the Sunday evening.

The coroner then explained the law and the duty of the magistrates, relative to riots. After a brief consultation the jury returned a verdict of 'Justifiable Homicide'.

The inquest on MacNamara followed a similar pattern, and his sister Bridget told the gathering he had gone off to Mr Oxendale's mill early that fateful day. He was brought home with a wound to his belly that was bleeding continuously. Despite medical attention he had died on the Monday afternoon. Once again, a verdict of 'Justifiable Homicide' was recorded.

It was noted at the hearing that other rioters taken to the House of Recovery were William Lancaster, aged twenty-five, a resident of Nugent Street, who had been shot in the chest; James Robert, a twenty-one-year-old weaver of Savoy Street, who had been shot in the forearm; Bryan Hodgson, aged thirty-six, a shoemaker of St Paul's Square, who was wounded in the lower part of the back; John Mercer, aged twenty-seven, a handloom weaver of Ribbleton Lane, who had been shot through the chest; and Lawrence Pilling, aged twenty-one, a weaver of Moss Rose Street, who had to have a leg amputated after a ball entered his leg below the knee, smashing the bone in a frightful manner.

Within the fortnight it was reported that two more of the rioters were dead. William Lancaster succumbed to his chest injuries after six days and John Mercer, the first to be shot, lingered for a further four days before expiring. Inquests into their deaths returned similar verdicts to those given at the former inquests.

Outside the public house nowadays simply called 1842 is a statue that reflects the events of Saturday, 13 August 1842. Fittingly, the Preston Martyrs Memorial was unveiled in August 1992 to mark the 150th anniversary of the tragic day, having been designed by sculptor Gordon Young.

Footnote: A full account titled 'Riot Act Read In Lune Street' appears in *Chilling True Tales of Old Preston: Book 2*, by Keith Johnson (1991).

Left: The Coroner Richard Palmer explained the law on riots.

Below: When the rioters faced the soldiers – a reminder of August 1842.

6. Crimean Cannons from Sebastopol

If you should approach Avenham Walk in Preston from the valley below, on either side of the terraced steps you will see a reminder of the Crimean War. Pointing out towards the River Ribble are two replicas of a pair of 36-lb Russian cannons, which were brought back from the Siege of Sebastopol in 1858 and presented to the town. The original cannons were mounted on stout wooden carriages with guns measuring 9 foot 6 inches in length, each having the Russian Imperial Eagle in bold relief on the upper portion. One of the trunnions carried the date stamp of '1835', while the other was dated '1837'.

The Preston-based 30th and 47th Regiments played a crucial part in the siege and eventual capture of the Russian port of Sebastopol, which virtually ended the conflict after the cruel winter of 1854–55. The original cannons were a familiar site at Avenham Park for generations, until they were melted down and used for the war effort in creating munitions for the Second World War.

In March 1854, the 30th and 47th Regiments were stationed at Gibralatar and Malta respectively. They were alerted for active service with an Anglo-French expedition to counter Russian expansion through the Balkans, towards Constantinople and the Mediterranean. Their objective was the great Russian Black Sea naval base of Sebastopol on the Crimean peninsula. Staging through Scutari on the Bosphorus and Varita in Bulgaria, both regiments landed in the Crimea in mid-September with the 2nd Division.

The Allies marched south towards Sebastopol and within days were confronted by the Russians, who were strongly entrenched covering the River Alma. A frontal attack was ordered, crossing the river and up a slope to capture the enemy redoubts. Advancing around the burning village of Bourliouk and fording the river under heavy artillery fire, the 30th and 47th moved steadily forward, side by side, to capture the centre of the Russian stronghold. Casualties of the 30th Foot at the Alma amounted to thirteen killed and sixty-six wounded, and those of the 47th were four killed and sixty-five wounded.

Sebastopol was laid to siege by late September and both the 30th and 47th Regiments, encamped on the Heights of Inkerman, were soon busily building siege works. In late October a detachment of the 30th Regiment formed part of the famous 'Thin Red Line' that repelled the Russian cavalry at the Battle of Balaclava. The following day, the 30th Regiment played a significant part in defeating an enemy reconnaissance force in the action known as 'Little Inkerman', sustaining thirty-two casualties during the action.

Early on the misty morning of 5 November 1854, the Russians made a determined advance from Sebastopol with 35,000 infantry and 135 guns as they targeted the Heights of Inkerman, held by the 2nd Division with fewer than 2,500 men and twelve guns. Lieutenant-Colonel Haly of the 47th Regiment, supported by two companies of his own, stood his ground stoutly while the rest of the division got under arms. Reinforced by men of the 30th and 47th Regiments, Haly led a gallant charge against the foremost Russians and cut three down before he was unhorsed and wounded. His rescue earned Private John McDermond of the 47th the Victoria Cross.

Meanwhile, the rest of the 2nd Division was fed forward to join the battle. Visibility was very poor and control almost impossible, so that battle was fought out at close quarters, often with the bayonet, as successive Russian regiments emerged from the mist to be engaged by the determined yet smaller parties of British infantry. Both the 30th and 47th Regiments made repeated bayonet charges, routing up to twelve times their number.

Eventually the Russians retreated, with the loss of some 12,000 men. The Battle of Inkerman became known as the soldiers' battle, costing the 30th Foot forty dead and ninety-three wounded, while the 47th lost twenty dead and forty-seven wounded. The epic battle is part of the heritage of the Duke of Lancaster's Regiment and the anniversary is celebrated each year as a regimental day.

A harsh winter was to follow, with the dreaded cholera leading to much sickness, and a violent storm in mid-November added to the miseries. The tempest led to the loss of over twenty supply ships, ravaged the tented camps and, when snow followed, life in the trenches was filled with suffering. Despite all this, the Allies maintained their siege of Sebastopol, and when spring arrived over 500 guns were in position to bombard the defences. By early June 1856 the enemy's advances were stormed and the 47th were part of the force that captured the Quarries position in fierce fighting, holding it with great gallantry against repeated counter-attacks. Early in September, the 30th attacked across

The scene at Redan after the capture of Sebastopol with a discarded cannon.

shell-swept open ground in a failed attempt on the Redan, suffering 165 casualties out of the 425 who left the trenches, including eleven of the sixteen officers.

Despite this temporary reversal, the Russian position was untenable and their evacuation of Sebastopol brought the war to a conclusion. The cost to the regiments was terrible; the 30th and 47th had, between them, lost over 1,000 of all ranks dead in the Crimea, mostly from disease rather than fighting. The battle honours of Alma, Inkerman and Sebastopol on the regimental colours record a campaign marked by great courage and endurance.

Original cannons on Avenham Walk, with Avenham Tower in the background.

The replica cannon.

7. Boer War – From Preston to South Africa

On 9 October 1899, war was declared between Great Britain, the Transvaal and the Orange Free State in South Africa. Ill feeling during the nineteenth century between the Dutch Afrikaners, known as the Boers, and British settlers came to a head when Paul Kruger, the President of South Africa, demanded the withdrawal of British troops from the Transvaal borders. The Boers had already migrated north to avoid being ruled by the British colony at the Cape of Good Hope. Gradually, the new Boer republics were annexed by Great Britain and when gold tempted thousands of British miners to the region conflict became inevitable.

The impact was later recorded by a soldier of the 1st South Lancashire Regiment who, along with members of the Loyal North Lancs Regiment, received the call to arms. The soldier described the scene in Preston as preparations began:

Our regiment, stationed at Preston, received orders to mobilize and prepare for active service, with the 1st Class Army Reserve ordered to rejoin by mid November with over 650 responding to the call. Consequently, all was commotion at Fulwood Barracks. Civilians were continually coming and going; some to see relatives and friends, others out of idle curiosity. During those last days the time was chiefly occupied in fitting clothing – khaki drab and organising kit and equipment. A number of the reserves were no sooner in the barracks than they were off home again in uniform, wanting to spend precious time with families before they departed.

On the Sunday prior to our departure the Mayor of Preston, James Yates Foster, visited the regiment at Fulwood Barracks, and spoke words of encouragement to the officers and men. The crowd of civilians on the barracks square then began to cheer and the officers and men were pleased with the response as they resolved to prove themselves worthy of their forefathers.

At last the day of our departure, the 30th of November, arrived and the send off we received from the public of Preston will ever be remembered as a red letter day for the regiments involved. As early as five o'clock that morning people had gathered at the barracks gates. Crowds lined the route from Fulwood, down Deepdale Road, along Church Street, up Fishergate, and on to the railway station.

The scenes that were enacted that day will live long in the memory of those who witnessed them. Here might be seen a soldier, his arms encircling a young child, with his wife clinging to him; there a sad looking fellow clasping his grey-haired mother to his breast, and whispering words of encouragement, although he knew this might be their final parting. Others were shaking hands and kissing people whom they had never before seen. Men and women laughed and wept alternately, and some young women became quite hysterical. The remarks passed often related to President Kruger, the most heard comments being 'Don't forget to make 'owd Kruger dance when tha' gets to Africa,' and 'Don't forget to bring 'owd Kruger's whiskers back.'

From the Town Hall to the railway station the crowd was dense, all struggling to get a glimpse of the boys in khaki. All along Fishergate the windows and balconies had been requisitioned, and were crowded with people waving flags and bunting of every description, and calling out 'good bye' to the soldiers below. Before we reached the station the vast multitude began to sing the national anthem. Having left the barracks in columns of four we were now in single file each soldier being cheered and handed gifts from the throngs of well wishers.

Patriotic music greeted us on the railway platform and once we had all quickly boarded the train we were off on our journey. On our arrival at Liverpool our regiment was marched from the railway sidings into the dock yard, and on to board the S.S. Canada. There were dense crowds in the dock yard hoping to say a fond farewell to the troops, but the soldiers were not allowed to leave their ships once aboard. At about 11 o'clock the next morning the anchor was weighed and we sailed away, leaving the shores of old England, perhaps for ever.

The Boer War called to arms regular battalions that had links back to Preston's early infantry soldiers and to local militia forces. Half of the 1st Loyal North Lancashire were sent from Cape Town to defend the diamond town of Kimberley, where they held out for over four months. They earned a unique battle honour for their performance. The relief force included the remaining companies of the 1st Loyal, who took part in the battles of Graspan and Modder River.

The Relief of Ladysmith saw the 1st South Lancashire Regiment in action at Spion Kop and Vaal Krantz, earning particular distinction at Pieters Hill, where the commanding officer was killed leading the charge that finally broke through to relieve Ladysmith. The anniversary of the relief – 27 February – is celebrated as a regimental day.

At the advance on Pretoria, the 1st East Lancashire Regiment marched on the city, earning high praise for their part in the actions at Jacobsdaal, Karee and the Zand River. Although the Boer field armies had been defeated, an arduous guerilla campaign lasted until 1902, with Lancashire soldiers taking part in many actions, often as mounted infantry.

Crowds greet the soldiers off to the Boer War on Fishergate.

Veterans pay their tribute in 1964.

The Boer War finally ended in late May 1902 by the signing of the Treaty of Vereeniging. Altogether the British suffered around 28,000 losses, while the Boers, although only losing 4,000 soldiers, lost up to 20,000 civilians from disease and starvation.

In early October 1904, Preston welcomed Major-General Kekewich to the town. The officer, who gained fame as the defender of Kimberley, visited the marketplace to unveil a monument erected in the memory of those officers and men of the Loyal North Lancashire Regiment who had fallen in the South African war.

A great civic and military procession took place and, despite a wet and windy day, a very large crowd witnessed the ceremony as Alderman Craven, the Mayor of Preston, accepted with pleasure, on behalf of the town, a memento of those brave men of the Loyal North Lancashire Regiment who had lost their lives.

The monument stands at 25 feet tall and was the work of local sculptor Mr T. Hodgkinson. The panels of the pedestal contain bronze inscription plates recording the names of the officers and men who lost their lives and other matters of interest relating to the regiment. The monument was entirely a regimental effort; no civilian had been allowed to subscribe.

Major-General Kekewich told those watching that in the course of the war seven officers and 117 men of the Loyal North Lancashire had upheld the honours and traditions of their regiment and sacrificed their lives. Both militia and volunteer battalions alike had bravely and courageously earned their place on the roll of honour. He concluded by saying, 'Long might this memorial remain here, as a record of true and loyal service, and as an incentive to all to emulate so noble an example.'

Sadly, he had no idea of the horrors that lay ahead for the soldiers of the regiment, and by 1925 the Boer War memorial had to be moved to Avenham Park as preparations got underway for the building of the cenotaph to mark the sacrifices made in the First World War that followed all too soon.

In February each year the Kimberley Parade takes place in Avenham Park in memory of the 1st Battalion of the LNLR and their heroic defence of Kimberley.

Time to pay tribute once more in February 1959.

The Boer War Memorial on Avenham Park nowadays.

8. Patriotic Pride in Preston Pals

Had you been a young man in Preston in August 1914 you may well have been swept along on the wave of patriotic pride as Earl Kitchener, the War Minister, laid plans to raise a new army of seventy infantry divisions. The Earl of Derby had suggested to Kitchener that men might be more willing to enlist in his new army if they could be assured of fighting alongside their own friends, neighbours and workmates.

Kitchener gave his blessing to the scheme, sanctioning local councils to raise what became known as the 'Pals battalions'. The new recruits were to be aligned with existing city or county regiments. Consequently, several battalions were formed with cotton brokers, tram drivers, office clerks and warehouse men, exchanging their uniforms, aprons or pinstriped suits for khaki, all eager to take up the challenge of overthrowing the kaiser and his vast armies, which were then occupying Belgium and threatening to conquer France.

The raising of the Preston Pals was the idea of Cyril Cartmell, son of the Mayor of Preston, Harry Cartmell. On the last day of August 1914 he placed an advert in the *Lancashire Daily Post*:

> It is proposed to form a company of young businessmen, clerks, etc, to be drawn from Preston and the surrounding districts, and be attached, if practicable, to a battalion of the Loyal North Lancashire Regiment. Will those who would like to join apply here any afternoon or evening this week – the earlier the better. Town Hall. Preston.

The local response, as indeed nationwide, was overwhelming and within a couple of days over 200 recruits had volunteered. This body was mainly made up of Preston folk, but also included were recruits from Blackpool, the Fylde and Chorley. A list of names and addresses that appeared in the *Preston Herald* on the following Wednesday showed the wide range of recruits all ready for departure. Over 166 of the men recruited had Preston addresses such as Friargate, Deepdale Road, Holmrook Road, Waterloo Terrace, Cannon Street, Garden Walk, London Road and Marsh Lane. It showed that all neighbourhoods had been touched by the effect of war and the need to serve the country.

The company made up of clerks, businessmen, journalists, architects, undergraduates and members of all the professions had been medically examined on the Sunday, with very few rejected. On the Monday they assembled for attestation at the Town Hall. At noon they were mustered and marched to the Public Hall, where a meal awaited for the young men about to leave town, and afterward each man received a packet of sandwiches for consumption on the forthcoming railway journey.

The Mayor of Preston addressed the gathering and expressed his gratification at finding that men coming from good families, comfortable homes, in good positions and

The local trams were advertising for recruits.

The scene at Preston railway station as the Preston Pals awaited departure.

in many cases the only sons of their parents, had responded so readily to the call. He concluded a much applauded speech by saying, 'There are some with us this afternoon who are men in inches, but only boys in years. I am asking the older men to keep an eye on them. Live clean and live straight, as well as shoot straight.'

A short, bright, impromptu concert followed, and the men assembled again and marched to the Market Square, where they paraded. On the Market Square and on the way to the station remarkably enthusiastic scenes were witnessed, as there was at the station itself, where hundreds of Prestonians flocked. The scenes were remarkably inspiring, with cheer after cheer following the special train as it moved away from the platform shortly after two o'clock. Little could quell the enthusiasm and there were busy scenes at the Town Hall where they were taking names for a second company of soldiers willing to do battle.

Kitchener and the British officials were in no doubt that it would take twelve months, possibly longer, before the Pals battalions could be expected to take their place alongside regular and territorial troops. The Preston Pals did their training at Belford, Tidworth and Swindon before crossing over to Boulogne in mid-July 1915. Once in France, a couple of months were spent in training for trench warfare and gas attacks.

In September 1915, exactly twelve months after their formation, the Preston Pals took a minor part in the Battle of Loos, and received their first casualties. Private Charles Pennington of Ribble Bank Street wrote home at the end of October to say, 'We have five killed and about 13 wounded.' By this time the folks back home were becoming all too aware of the dreadful reality of war as local papers reported the losses. Each week obituaries of the fallen soldiers appeared in the press with details of their school, church and work associations prior to the conflict. The lad you had played football or cricket with, or played in the cobbled street with had died on some foreign battle field. Husbands, sons, brothers and nephews had fallen in action.

Following the opening battles, both the Allies and the Germans found themselves firmly in a deadlock of trench warfare. Long lines of trenches stretched across France and Flanders from the Swiss border to the Channel coast. Allied attempts in 1915 had failed to break through, mainly due to a lack of men and ammunition; but, there was confidence that in the summer of 1916 all this would change, thanks to Kitchener's new army.

On the first day of July 1916 the big push was underway as the British infantry divisions attacked the Germans along a 15-mile front. The troops, many consisting of Pals battalions, faced the battle with much confidence. Sadly, within minutes of leaving the trenches the soldiers walked into a hail of machine gun and sniper fire. The dead lay strewn across the muddy fields as many British soldiers failed to advance even a few yards from their own lines. It was a traumatic day for Kitchener's Army, two years in the making, and by nightfall a casualty list of over 60,000 troops spelt out the horror of the day.

Within days the town of Accrington heard the sad news that the Accrington Pals had suffered horrendous casualties, with over 235 officers and men having been killed and another 350 wounded within a matter of minutes.

The Preston Pals had been scheduled to take part in an assault against German lines in the late afternoon, but the failure of the earlier attacks led to cancellation of that offensive. In spite of the first day of the Battle of the Somme, the British offensive pressed on and more infantry battalions were thrown into the attack. The Preston Pals were engaged in the Battle of the Somme throughout July, taking part in many a desperate fight. By mid-July barely 500 riflemen out of an original strength of 900 remained. During August and September 1916, the 7th Battalion of the Loyals served in Flanders, only to return to the Somme again as that battle entered its final phase. In reality, after the Battle of the Somme what remained of many Pals battalions were either disbanded or reformed with men from differing locations.

Much of my information about the Preston Pals comes from an old soldier's remembrance of the historic conflict over seventy years after the event. He went on to refer to some of the losses that the Preston Pals suffered, recalling how the vicar of St George's had lost his son, Lieutenant Maurice Bannister; how the son of Alderman Hugh Rain had also fallen; and that Harold Fazackerley of Ashton had won the Military Cross before being killed in action. He also remembered one of the last surviving members of the Preston Pals, James Collier Nickeas, who was on that *Preston Herald* list as living on Plungington Road, Fulwood, and who had died in 1986 in a Barrow hospital, aged ninety-three.

Of course, the cenotaph now looks over the Market Square where those brave soldiers of the Preston Pals first paraded over 100 years ago. Preston without a doubt remains eternally proud of the Preston Pals and aware of the sacrifice paid by so many local families.

Those brave Preston Pals were remembered again in 2015 by members of the Lancashire Infantry Museum in full battledress in the Market Square.

9. Letters from the Western Front

There are many letters from the First World War that became part of our military heritage. These precious communications were greeted with delight by both those in the theatre of war and those who waited and worried back home.

Among those brave soldiers on the Western Front was Private Roland Shawcross, who was a reporter for the *Lancashire Daily Post* before he enlisted with the Preston Pals in the 7th Battalion of the Loyals. Who better, then, to describe the scene from the trenches? In a letter to a friend back in Blackburn, the son of Mr and Mrs Shawcross had this to say about the Christmas he had endured of 1915:

On the part of the frontline we are occupying there was no truce. The message of peace and goodwill was not exchanged between the British and German troops. Amongst the men the opinion was frequently expressed that we had not come out in order to shake hands with the Huns. Neither was there any desire to exchange friendly greetings with a foe who as individuals stoop to such fiendish devices as the use of explosive bullets. If those at home could see our men not merely put out of action but unnecessarily shattered and maimed as a result of those bullets they would realise that a truce even at Christmas was scarcely appropriate. So as to our Christmas along the British front our troops gathered as equals, celebrating the birth of the Saviour of the World. Men united together, who have made sacrifices in the past, and are still prepared to make them in the future, with the knowledge that through those sacrifices a nation's glorious and stainless heritage will be handed on to future generations.

Thoughts of our island home filled many a soldier's heart in the trenches of France this Christmas. Many a happy vision of the past was crowded on our memories, and many a yearning to sit round the Yuletide fire, to hear once again the merry laughter of children, to occupy that vacant seat at the old home gatherings.

Yet duty held thousands away in foreign lands amidst the horror of war. The gathering at which I was present was held in an old barn behind the front line. Festoons hung from the rafters along with Chinese lanterns. A charcoal fire burned brightly, despite the protestations of an old French woman, who feared her barn might be burnt to the ground. Fruit, plum pudding, cakes, and all delicacies associated with Christmas were upon the table. The men bronzed with months of campaigning sat around the fire truly enjoying the brief respite from duty. It was a scene which will never be forgotten. Choruses we had a plenty. How strangely appropriate that popular song 'Keep the Home Fires Burning' seemed that night, sung by men who for six months had never seen the home fires they love so well!

Never was there a more varied programme of impromptu, yet possessed with a strange grandeur and pathos. It was close on midnight when that merry party broke up. All agreed it had been a success but could not be compared to a Christmas on English soil.

Duties had to be carried out the next day, and the day after we were once more on our way to the trenches traversing roads in many places completely under water, due to heavy rains. It was a hazardous journey to the frontline exposed not only to enemy artillery, but to machine guns and rifle fire. Bullets whistled all around, ploughing up the mud in many instances practically at our feet. Over ponds, deep dikes, and ditches we wended our way on narrow planks until our destination was reached.

The following day our front line was rather heavily shelled, but we were let off with two casualties. Owing to the winter conditions it is seldom that troops are stationed in the front line for more than 48 hours. In the daytime owing to the keen vigilance of the German snipers we are unable to move about. And only yesterday morning a Captain in the battalion was killed. Although we have suffered many casualties, our men have had the best of luck, especially when one considers the risk from day to day. Take for instance our last relief, when we were openly exposed to the German front line. A machine gun suddenly opened fire, and bullets flew fast and furious all around, yet there was not a single casualty.

Then again, there is a marked change in the men, who are now very cool and collected. Only last night we were called on to work in the front line. With great planks on their shoulders the men went over open country, laughing and jesting as they foundered in the deepest of mud and water, heedless of the danger they were facing. They work on the top of the parapet in a manner which would suggest that shells, bombs and bullets were unknown.

On another occasion a shell burst practically on one of our men. When the smoke had cleared he was still standing unscathed, calmly inquiring if anyone was hit. In contrast to such miraculous escapes men have been killed away down in the reserves by stray shots, a fact which naturally originates the idea of fatalism. The spirit of the men is magnificent. Like all Tommies. They may grouse on occasions, but for cheerfulness and fortitude they are incomparable. There is a natural longing after six months of warfare to have a glimpse of Old England once again, but they wait patiently for their turn to come.

The letters sent by Private Rowland Shawcross were no doubt cherished by his family and friends and they helped to paint the picture of life in the trenches for the folks back home.

In February 1916 it was reported in the *Lancashire Daily Post* that Private Shawcross was in hospital in France suffering from trench foot. Happily, in 2016 following research by Mike Hill, the communities editor of the *Lancashire Post*, we know that he became Corporal Ronald Waldo Shawcross, that he survived the war, was married to Edith McKeand in Blackburn in July 1917, and lived a long life, dying in Worcester in 1978 aged eighty-four.

Thanks to research by Roger Goodwin of the Lancashire Infantry Museum we now know the officer to whom Roland refers to was Captain M. Thomas, who was shot by a German sniper and died a few hours later. The front line trench was between the villages of Richebourg l'Avoue and Neuve Chapelle – the scene of a major battle earlier that year.

PTE. S. E. GLAISTER.

Private Sidney E Glaister, of the Liverpool Regt., whose home is at 22, St. Paul's-square, Preston, has been wounded by a rifle bullet in the shoulder and shrapnel in the left arm and right ankle. He is still in France, and making good progress. Before joining the Army at the end of August, 1914, he was a teacher at Woolton Church Day Schools, Liverpool. Previously he was a choirboy and scholar of St. Paul's and later was for some years at Preston Grammar School.

PTE. R. BAINES.

Mrs. T. Baines, of the De Tabley Arms, Ribchester Bridge (late of the Victoria and Station Hotel, Preston), has received a notification that her elder son, Private Reginald Baines, of the "Preston Pals" Company, L.N.L. Regt., was killed at the front on November 17th. His company officer writes:—

"He was so full of life, and noble, and beloved by officers and men wherever he went."

Lance-Corpl. David W. Taylor, one of his chums, says he fell just after a successful advance, and was killed in a dug-out along with one of the officers. "You have the deep sympathy of all that remain of the Preston Pals."

SERGT. JOHN NUTTALL.

Mrs. Nuttall, 32, Park-road, Preston, has received an intimation of the death in action in France, on August 8th, of her son, Sergeant John Nuttall (24), of the L.N.L. Regiment. Signalling Officer J. B. Blakeway writes:—

"Sergt. Nuttall was killed by a shell on the morning of the 8th, whilst writing a letter to you. I enclose the letter. He was what I would term a real soldier, and was very valuable to me. I have missed his help greatly, and I can assure you he always did his duty and never showed fear." The letter referred to is as follows:—"My dear parents,—I thought I would write you a few lines to let you know I am still quite all right. I may tell you that we are still having some lovely weather. We are in a very hot shop, and the sooner we get from here the better. By the way——" At this point the letter abruptly ends. He was formerly a weaver at Messrs. Paley's mill, London-road.

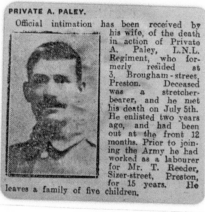

PRIVATE A. PALEY.

Official intimation has been received by his wife, of the death in action of Private A. Paley, L.N.L. Regiment, who formerly resided at 3, Brougham-street, Preston. Deceased was a stretcher-bearer, and he met his death on July 5th. He enlisted two years ago, and had been out at the front 12 months. Prior to joining the Army he had worked as a labourer for Mr. T. Reeder, Sizer-street, Preston, for 15 years. He leaves a family of five children.

Above: A bleak Christmas scene on the Western Front for many.

Left: Among the victims were these four local heroes.

10. The Munition Lasses

To mark the 100th anniversary of the birth of Dick, Kerrs Ladies football team a magnificent granite plaque was unveiled outside Deepdale, the home of Preston North End, in 2017. It was in no small way that local lady Gail Newsham contributed to the creation of this slice of Preston's heritage. Her book *In a League of Their Own* (1997) and her tireless research were the source of much interest in the tale of the Lancashire lasses from the munition factory.

The coming of the First World War saw thousands of women employed in factories producing munitions, and few places were busier than the engineering works of Dick Kerr Co. Ltd on Strand Road. The company had been founded by William Bruce Dick and John Kerr from Scotland in 1903 when they took over the factory to manufacture trams and electrical equipment. As the First World War progressed the nation was desperate for ammunition and so the premises were converted into a munitions factory.

While thousands of men were fighting on the bloody battlefields of the Western Front, large numbers of women were drafted in to work in the munition factories. These women became known as 'munitionettes'. Working long hours, the women were exposed to dangerous conditions involving chemicals and heavy machinery.

The most visible side effect of munitions work was seen by those women who spent their days filling shells with TNT. This highly explosive chemical often caused the hair and the skin of the women to turn yellow. This visible sign of toxic jaundice earned the women the nickname 'Canaries' and in extreme cases led to a premature death.

Set to emerge from the situation were a group of women who would leave their own heritage to the cause of ladies football. As the First World War progressed ladies football teams were being formed up and down the country. Their involvement in football was seen as an opportunity to raise much needed funds for local charities.

In 1915, ladies who worked in the Preston Records Office formed a team that played a number of matches locally to raise funds for the wounded soldiers being treated at the temporary hospital on Moor Park. The team attracted large crowds as they turned out in their natty striped shirts, long black stockings, short skirts and mob caps. Among their ranks was sixteen-year-old Elsie Arnold a dashing centre forward who would later play for Dick, Kerr Ladies.

The girls at Dick, Kerrs were encouraged to take up the sport by their male counterparts and this led to the memorable Christmas Day match of 1917 against the ladies of the Arundel Coulthard Foundry. A crowd in excess of 10,000 gathered, a hard fought 4-0 victory was gained and £600 was collected on the gate for charity. The man who would become their mentor and manager was Albert Frankland, a draughtsman at Dick Kerrs who oversaw two tours of France, the first in 1920. That year they played on Boxing Day at Goodison Park against St Helens Ladies, watched by a crowd of 53,000 as they gained a 4-0 victory.

The tribute to Dick, Kerrs Ladies footballers was unveiled in 2017 at Deepdale.

The ladies of Dick, Kerrs took on the world of football.

The progress of ladies football received a blow in December 1921 when the FA imposed a ban on the womens game being played on the grounds of their member clubs. The FA said, 'The game of football is quite unsuitable for females and ought not to be encouraged.'

Despite the sport being frowned upon the Dick, Kerrs Ladies overcame the FA obstacles to continue playing and their popularity and success continued. A reflection of the esteem surrounding them was a report in the national press in May 1924 that described Miss Lily Parr as the cleverest girl footballer in the kingdom, with her team manager Albert Frankland describing her thus:

> I can best describe her abilities by referring you to the opinion of men like Billy Meredith, Bobby Walker and Teddy Vizard, who have all described her as a most wonderful girl with a terrific left foot drive. The Americans described her as 'the girl with the wicked kick'. She has scored from her outside left position in 96 matches playing for us a total of 249 goals. I make bold to say that she can centre a ball on any full size ground in England as well as any of our star players; in fact, she has done so already. I describe her as the most wonderful girl footballer in the world.

In mid-October 1957 Walter Pilkington, the sports editor of the *Lancashire Evening Post*, wrote the following after the recent death of Alfred Frankland, aged seventy-four:

> He was a football pioneer who had, at one time, everyman's hand raised against him in official quarters. His crime was that it was not thought fitting for women to be seen in public wearing shorts in those less enlightened times. They could rightly claim to be world champions having defeated teams all over the country, successfully toured the United States and Canada and won international fixtures with France. In four seasons they lost only four times. In the 1920-21 season they played 59 matches winning all but one match which was drawn. His guidance ensured that everyone soon heard of the likes of Lily Parr, Alice Kell and Florrie Retford.

Praise indeed for the manager and the team that would continue to play until 1965 when they folded. They had raised countless thousands for charity, entertained vast crowds and been inspirational in the popularity and growth of ladies football. Their contribution to the heritage of football, born during difficult military days, is worthy of the Deepdale monument that recognises their outstanding deeds. The Women's Football Association was eventually formed in 1969, and in 1971 the FA officially recognised ladies football and the exploits of Dick, Kerrs Ladies live on in the memories of many.

11. The Fallen Football Heroes

In late October 2018 another memorial was unveiled outside the Deepdale ground of Preston North End FC in remembrance of the twenty-one former first team, reserve and amateur players who were registered at one time with PNE and lost their lives during the conflicts of the First World War. Not only does the memorial display their names, but also their regiments, when they died and their last resting place. Present at this unveiling was the PNE historian Ian Rigby whose painstaking research helped to make this tribute to the fallen possible.

Like people from every walk of life many footballers paid the ultimate price, and their sacrifice is part of the heritage of the football community who mourned their loss. Each of the named players left behind memories of their football playing days.

Private Alfred Lorrimer, Private James Chalmers, Private Thomas Henry Knibbs, Private William James Cox, Gunner Frank James Hesham, Lance Corporal John Barbour, Sapper Thomas Blakeley, Private William Walter Gerrish, Private Tom Pemberton Saul, Captain Thomas Sowerby Rowlandson, Sergeant William Ernest Meyler, Private Benjamin Haigh Green, Private John Ford, Private Frank Shanley, Sergeant Thomas Schaill, Private William Kirby, Sergeant Arthur Beadsworth, Sergeant Frederick John Griffiths, Private Walter Cook, Sapper William Sergeant and Gunner Herbert Bradley had all worn a Preston North End shirt at some stage of their football career. The losses felt by Preston North End were mirrored throughout the Football League, with no less than 296 British footballers being killed during the First World War.

The Preston Army Pay Office girls also took to the football field in 1918.

The plaque at Deepdale in memory of the PNE ex-footballers killed.

Preston North End maintained their First Division status after the First World War and reached the FA Cup final of 1922.

12. Streets of Remembrance – Lest We Forget

The recent naming of the new Broughton Bypass to James Towers Way recognises the achievements of the late James Towers as a holder of the Victoria Cross for his bravery in 1918. It shows that Preston has never been lacking in its recognition of the brave military, and the streets of Preston are steeped in memories of battles fought. Back in the seventeenth century, when the Civil War dominated life, Preston was a Royalist stronghold and the skirmishes that took place in the town are remembered in our street names. When the Duke of Hamilton's forces clashed with Oliver Cromwell's army under the leadership of General John Lambert on Ribbleton Moor in August 1648, their names were set to live on down the centuries. We have a Cromwell Road, Cromwell Street, Oliver's Place and indeed a Hamilton Road, Lambert Road and Langdale Road, all carrying the names of generals who led the fighting, while Stuart Road recalls the Royalists.

In the eighteenth century, thousands of pro-Catholic Jacobite rebels were forced to surrender in the marketplace. Many of their lives were cut short, but their names have spanned the centuries. The Church of the English Martyrs stands on Gallows Hill where many of the surrendering soldiers were beheaded. In the vicinity of the church are a number of streets that carry a martyr's name: Kenmure Place and Derwentwater Place are a reminder of two young soldiers dedicated to the Stuart cause, who were both beheaded at Tower Hill, London, in 1716; Butler Place and Muncaster Road are named in remembrance of William Butler, a conspicuous papist; and Roger Muncaster, an attorney, both of whom were hanged on Gallows Hill in 1716. Likewise, Richard Shuttleworth and William Arkwright, who were also hung and decapitated, have their names on Shuttleworth Road and Arkwright Road to remind us of those cruel days. Lockhart Road is so called in honour of Captain Philip Lockhart of Carnforth, who was shot in Preston in December 1715 along with three others. Lovat Road gets its name from Lord Lovat, who was connected with the first rebellion in 1715 before deserting to the opposite side and being pardoned. Thirty years on he was back with the Jacobites and, after being imprisoned, he was beheaded on Tower Hill. Other streets that get their name from the 1745 conflict include Elcho Street and Elcho Terrace, a reminder of Lord Elcho, a colonel at the time, and Elgin Street is named after the Burgh of Elgin where Bonnie Prince Charlie prepared for the bloody Battle of Culloden in April 1746.

The battles at sea have also left their legacy in our thoroughfares, with the likes of Rodney Street named after Admiral George Brydges Rodney, famous for clashes with Dutch, French and Spanish fleets, and Vernon Street named in tribute to Admiral Edward Vernon who captured Portobello in 1739 following a battle with the Spanish fleet. That other admiral, Horatio Nelson, was so good we used his name twice – the old Nelson Street and present-day Nelson Terrace – and, of course, his battles are remembered with Trafalgar Terrace and Nile Street. That other historical great, the Duke of Wellington, proved popular in the Ashton area of the city with a Wellington Street, Road and Terrace. One of Wellington's great commanders was Lord Hill, a general of distinction whose name graces Hill Street and Hill Place. Quite naturally, we also remember the Battle of Waterloo (1815) with Waterloo Road.

When the Crimean War was fought in the middle of the nineteenth century there was massive growth taking place in the industrial life of the town and many streets were

Above left: English Martyrs RC Church built on Gallows Hill.

Above right: Lord Lovat executed on Tower Hill.

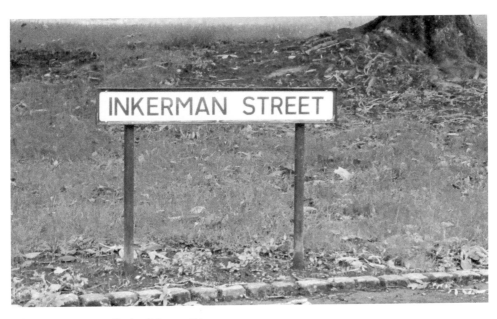

Inkerman Street recalls the Crimean War.

named in recognition of the heroic soldiers of the time. Raglan Street carries the name of the commander in chief of the British forces, and Campbell Street carries the name of the officer who succeeded him. Cardigan Street remembers Lord Cardigan, who led and survived the Charge of the Light Brigade, and Wetherall Street remembers an officer who fell in the charge. The fighting over the River Alma produced a hero in Delacy Evans and his name adorns two streets in the Plungington area. Cambridge Street honours the Duke of Cambridge, a young and successful commander in the Crimea, and Villiers Street pays tribute to George Frederick Villiers who was Secretary of State at the time. Inkerman Street is yet another reminder of the battles of the Crimea when the Russian foe was defeated.

Havelock Street and Terrace were named in honour of Sir Henry Havelock, a battle-hardened veteran who was a leading figure in the Indian Mutiny and the Relief of Lucknow. Sir Charles Napier was similarly honoured with Napier Street, as was Lord Ripon with Ripon Street, recognising the Viceroy of India, while other generals from the India troubles were remembered when they named Hammond Street and Miles Street. Death in Khartoum made Major General Charles Gordon a national martyr and Gordon Street was given his name.

It was an Egyptian mutiny that took place in Alexandria that led to the naming of Seymour Street and Willis Road, with an admiral and a general being thus remembered, while Viscount Garnet Wolseley earned much recognition with Wolseley Road, Terrace, Place and Court honouring the commander in chief.

When they developed the fields around Meadow Street into a housing estate, Prussia was threatening Denmark and subsequently regions in the news were used with the naming of Holstein Street, Jutland Street, Schelswig Street and Danewerke Street adding a foreign flavour to the area. The Boer War at the dawn of the twentieth century led to the naming of property in the Tulketh Brow area with Mafeking Street (after the siege in that town), and Ladysmith Street, Kimberley Street, Colenso Road and Belmont Street all getting names from battle grounds during that particular conflict. While the Earl of Dundonald is not forgotten with Dundonald Street named after the man who led the cavalry brigade into Ladysmith. Arnhem Road commemorates the Battle of Arnhem and Dunkirk Avenue reminds us of the spirit instilled by Sir Winston Churchill, whose name is on the street signs of Churchill Road in Brookfield, while his father Lord Randolph Churchill is recalled with Churchill Street. And if you ever wondered what happened to German Street, it was renamed Owen Street after the First World War by the patriotic Prestonians; however, it was never actually named after our then enemies at all, but after Thomas German, a much admired former Mayor of Preston. Certainly, the battles of old have played their part in Preston street names, why else would we have a Zulu Terrace on Ripon Street? It is apparent that Preston has always acknowledged the achievements of those who have fought in conflicts, be they at home or on foreign fields.

13. Raising a Glass to the Returning Heroes

Many a member of the armed forces while on duty abroad dreamt of the day they might return and drink a pint of their favourite beer. Fortunately, for those exiled Prestonians there was never a shortage of alehouses happy to welcome them home, with an added bonus, perhaps, of the fact that quite a few carried a name steeped in military heritage, with historical events and names having found an abiding place on the signboard of local public houses.

There was at one time in Vat Street an Allies Inn, commemorating the allies of the Crimean War. That campaign also giving us an Alma Inn and a Sebastopol Inn, with Lord Raglan being honoured by a beerhouse in Harrington Street.

The Battle of Waterloo has also been prolific in public house nomenclature, and once again Preston remembered this historical event. Only in 1984 did the well-remembered Waterloo Hotel on Friargate meet its own Waterloo. At one time four local inns carried the name of the Duke of Wellington. Those Wellington Inns on Bedford Street and Fletcher Road are long gone, but the Wellington Inn on Glovers Court and the Wellington Hotel on Tulketh Road still serve ale and remind us of the famous victory of 1815. The current inn sign of the Wellington Inn, where ale has been served since 1839, portrays an image of the former leading military and political figure who was twice prime minister. There was also an Iron Duke public house situated on North Road, which carried the nickname often used to describe the Duke of Wellington.

Throughout Lancashire the name of Lord Nelson was remembered in seventeen inn names and Preston's stood on North Road at the junction of Sedgewick Street. Ribbleton Lane provided us with a Nelson's Monument, while an inn in Bushell Street carried the name of Napoleon. Both Nelson and Napoleon, cast in stone, stood aloft of the Port Admiral Hotel in Lancaster Road South. Alas, they along with the mysterious lady said to be Lady Hamilton were removed from Preston's skyline in 1969 prior to the inn's demolition as the town made way for the ring road.

Soldier and explorer Sir John Franklin, General Sir Charles Napier, General Codrington and General Lee all had their names above local public houses, and the General Havelock on Plungington Road survived until 2009.

While back in early Victorian times you could have a beer in the Oliver Cromwell in Shepherd Street, which carried his name until 1866 when it became the Soldier's Return. Some might lament the loss of the Fortunes Of War, an inn that stood on Mill Bank, Church Street, until it was demolished in late 1968, or the Jolly Tars on Mount Pleasant or, indeed, the Jolly Sailor that stood on Stanley Street. Many a sailor thought the Anchor's Weighed Inn on Ribbleton Lane had an appropriate name, as did the former Hearts of Oak, a name bestowed on early seafaring vessels and the title of the official march of the Royal Navy, which stands on Adelphi Street and is nowadays named the Vinyl Tap.

One of the more recent examples of a local inn with military connections was the Falkland Heroes, which opened in Tanterton in 1983 and was visited by a number of those who served in the Falklands War; sadly the inn was burnt down in 2002. The aptly named Royal Garrison situated close to Fulwood Barracks was a handy location for thirsty soldiers down the years, but this public house put the shutters up in 2012. And yes, we did very briefly have a public house named the Toy Soldier, built on the new Deepdale Retail Park in 1998, but it closed in 2006 after a troubled existence.

To this day the Army & Navy, which dates back to 1867 when Thomas Turner was landlord, before thoughts of a Royal Air Force and aerial warfare, still stands on Meadow Street and welcomes veterans of the RAF along with soldiers and sailors.

The Wellington Inn on Glovers Court, serving ale since 1839.

The Royal Garrison was popular with soldiers from Fulwood Barracks.

The General Havelock on Plungington Road, pictured *c.* 1989. *Inset*: The inn sign of the Army & Navy on Meadow Street, a public house that dates back to 1867, well before battles in the sky.

14. Why War?

In late April 1939, as the world stood once more on the brink of war, a painting was being exhibited in a Royal Academy Exhibition in London that caught the eye of former Mayor of Preston, James Harrison, chairman of the Preston Art Committee, and Mr Sydney H. Paviere, the art director and curator of the Harris Art Gallery.

The picture titled *Why War?* was understandably topical at the time and was by the artist Charles Spencelayh, who was born in Kent in 1865. Two of his previous works *Smile* and *His Favourite* being among the collection of the Townley Hall Art Gallery.

The oil painting shows the interior of an ordinary working-class home with the figure of an elderly man seated on a chair with his hands clasped, obviously asking himself the question that is the title of the picture. On the table near to him is his gas mask, and thrown carelessly on to another chair is a copy of a newspaper with the headline 'Premier Flying to Hitler'. A print of the picture *The Death of Nelson* by Arthur William Devis, an artist with strong links to Preston, hangs on the wall where the old man's steel helmet also has a place. Various articles within the room include a grandfather clock, tall boy, heavily framed pictures and the design of the furniture are all in character with the age of the occupant of the room.

Delighted with their discovery, the two art enthusiasts from Preston agreed to purchase the painting for £315 (equal to £20,000 these days) and to display it to future generations of Preston folk, many of whom would ponder over the thoughts behind the title. The painting was given the Royal Academy's Picture of the Year award in 1939. Charles Spencelayh died in June 1958, aged ninety-two, and his masterpiece *The Old Dealer* was sold at auction at Sotheby's in 2009 for £345,000.

Ironically, the *Why War?* painting only arrived in Preston at the end of August 1939, just a few days before war broke out. It was revealed that the funding of the painting, which measures 36 inches by 28 inches, had been provided from the endowment funds of the Harris trustees with no cost to the ratepayers. Plans were already underway to remove many of the museum's treasures to a place of safety and security. On display to this day, it is a thought-provoking picture that catches the eye on a visit to the Harris Art Gallery and is part of our military heritage.

Within the Harris Museum and Art Gallery there is a roll of honour remembering all those who died in the First World War. It contains the names of 1,956 men from Preston that were registered, which are inscribed on marble tablets on the two main staircases on the ground floor. It is thought that at least another 400 victims of that war were not registered by their families. No memorial nor roll of honour was produced for those killed in the Second World War, but the war memorial on the Market Square is also dedicated to those victims. A folder containing the names of all those who lost their lives since 1945 in the various conflicts is available to view in the Harris Community Library.

The thought-provoking painting *Why War?*, purchased in 1939.

The First World War roll of honour in the Harris Museum.

15. The Sacrifice of Our Sailors

The news received in Preston in mid-October 1939 reflected the heritage of war and was a warning as to what lay ahead in the months and years of the Second World War. Many local families had waved off their sons, daughters, husbands and wives as they left these shores to engage in combat on land and on sea.

On 14 October 1939 the battleship *Royal Oak* was sunk at anchor in the naval base of Scapa Flow in Orkney, Scotland, by the German submarine U-47. At dead of night the U-boat fired two starboard torpedoes at the vessel, which was anchored at the extreme end of the harbour, of which one hit the bow. Twenty minutes later the U-boat fired three, possibly four, further torpedoes and these caused the twenty-five-year-old ship to capsize and sink.

Of the ship's crew of 1,234 men and youths, no less than 833 were killed that night, or died later from their wounds. Quite naturally, there was great anxiety throughout the nation as families waited to hear news of relatives. A couple of days later the headlines in the *Lancashire Evening Post* reflected the perils of war with news and pictures of a victim and a survivor.

The Cairns family, who lived in Ringwood Road, Deepdale, received a telegram from the Admiralty that simply read: 'Regret to inform you that your son, John Cairns, died at sea.' John Cairns, aged nineteen, was a former scholar at St Ignatius School. He had enlisted around a year earlier and after training on HMS *Victory*, followed by service on HMS *Rodney*, he had spent a few months aboard the *Royal Oak*. His devastated parents and three sisters were stunned by the awful news.

A contrasting telegram was received at the Hughlock family home in Crowle Street, Preston: 'Pleased to inform you Marine William Hughlock is a survivor from the Royal Oak.' A native of Preston, the eighteen-year-old marine had worked as a labourer after leaving the Church of England school of St Mary's and had joined the Royal Marines eighteen months earlier. His mother was relieved to hear the news after having spent a couple of days fearing the worst.

A week later William Hughlock stepped off a train at Preston railway station to be greeted by relatives who he thought he would never see again. Once back at the family home the Royal Navy marine told the tale of his miraculous escape, of how as the ship was sinking in Scapa Flow he had escaped through a porthole in his pyjamas before swimming 4 miles to the shore. The ship had slid under the water within ten minutes of the second explosion and as it plunged fuel oil gushed from its funnel and the surface of the sea became black and sticky, with many men choking to death and others crushed by a drifter attending at the side. He had then been in the middle of an air raid on the naval base and was later involved in a train crash along with 300 other survivors of the sinking. He was home on a fortnight's leave having crammed a lifetime of adventure and narrow escapes into a few days.

For the Preston folk back home, their thoughts were with the Preston sailors throughout the war, where both triumphs and tragedies were commonplace. The exploits of Keith Mayor, who was just sixteen years old at the outbreak of war and joined the Home Guard prior to enlisting in the Royal Navy in June 1942, were particularly harrowing. After ten months' service he was involved in Operation Checkmate, which was attempting to sabotage German convoys on the Norwegian coast. Unfortunately his party encountered difficulties and were captured. After being detained at Grini he was transferred to the infamous Sachsenhausen concentration camp. He was treated harshly there and a number of his colleagues faced the firing squad. He was later moved to the notorious Bergen-Belsen camp. Sadly, he died there at the beginning of April 1945, with British troops just a few miles from Belsen. It later emerged that he had caught typhus at Belsen and been taken out and shot in the forehead.

In April 1947 he was granted a posthumous mention in despatches for great fortitude and resolution while in the hands of the enemy. His name is engraved on one of the panels of the Plymouth Naval Memorial and is forever impressed in the history of Preston's brave serviceman.

PRESTON VICTIM OF ROYAL OAK DISASTER

MR. and Mrs. J. Cairns, of Ringwood - road, Deepdale, Preston, received news from the Admiralty yesterday that their only son, 19-year-old John Cairns, was a victim of the Royal Oak disaster.

The telegram read: "Regret to inform you that your son, John Cairns, died at sea."

Formerly a scholar at St. Ignatius' School, John enlisted about 12 months ago, and received his early training on H.M.S. Victory, after which he was transferred to H.M.S. Rodney.

J. Cairns.

He had been in Royal Oak only a few months.

Mr. and Mrs. Cairns, who were prostrated

18-YEAR-OLD PRESTON SURVIVOR

Pleased to inform you Marine William Hughlock is survivor from Royal Oak.—Marines, Portsmouth.

THIS telegram, delivered at 4 a.m. yesterday at the home of Mr. and Mrs. J. Hughlock, of 14, Crowle-street, Preston, relieved the agony of mind they had been in since 1 p.m. the previous day, when they heard of the sinking of the Royal Oak.

Their son joined the Royal Marines about 18 months ago, and after coming home on leave last Whitsuntide, was appointed to the Royal Oak, the first ship on which he has been stationed.

A native of Preston, he is 18 years of age, and received his urge to join the Forces

Marine William Hughlock

Contrasting news of the perils at sea during war.

16. Weapons of War

There are some 10,000 folk employed in Lancashire by BAE Systems, a company that has been at the forefront of aircraft technology for decades. Among the roots of this business was the Preston-based English Electric, which owed its development to W. B. Dick & John Kerr who came to town to take over the North of England Carriage & Iron Company in Strand Road in 1897. Dick, Kerr & Co. Ltd, who had been long established in Kilmarnock, soon had the workforce of over 800 busily employed in making tramcars and railway carriages.

Before long the English Electric Co. would also be formed, with its new factory also along Strand Road. During the First World War the workforce showed their versatility by building seaplanes and flying boats for the Royal Navy. Besides an army of munition workers producing guns and shells from 1914 they produced the first of some sixty Preston-built Felixstowe F3 flying boats in early 1918 – a time when German U-boats threatened to rule the waves.

Between the wars the English Electric Co. produced the Wren auxiliary engine glider for the Air Ministry, the success of which led to the Air Ministry awarding the Preston factory a contract to build the Kingston flying boat. The Kingston had its first flight in May 1924 and led to further boats being built as the design progressed.

By 1938 the employees of the English Electric Co., with an aerodrome at Salmlesbury and premises on Strand Road in Preston, were awarded a contract for the manufacture of seventy-five Hampden bombers. The Air Ministry were quick to utilise the facilitates for the flight testing and assembly of the aircraft. The Hampden, originally designed and developed by the Handley Page Co., was a twin-engine medium bomber employed by the RAF.

Altogether some 770 Hampden would come off the Preston production lines by March 1942. It meant round the clock working for Preston folk, with twelve-hour shifts. When production ceased on the Hampden they began building the Halifax, a four-engine heavy bomber, again designed by the Handley Page Co. Over 2,100 of these aircraft were built at Strand Road.

In 1944, realising the need for their own design of aircraft, English Electric set up a design office in Preston on the old Barton Motors site on the corner of Corporation Street. In 1945, the first English Electric De Havilland Vampire jet aircraft was flown from the Salmlesbury airfield as they worked to fulfil orders for 300 of them. Not long after, the company acquired the Warton Aerodrome and established design facilities there.

What followed next was the development of the Canberra, which was introduced to service with the RAF in 1951. This jet-powered bomber went on to great popularity, with hundreds coming off the production line. It was followed by the Lightning, a supersonic fighter aircraft that could travel at twice the speed of sound. It took five years of

Dick, Kerrs factory on Strand Road in 1915 with over 2,000 employed on war work.

Halifax bombers off the war production line at Strand Road.

The supersonic Lightning is on display at Salmlesbury these days.

development to perfect this lethal weapon of war, which entered service with the RAF in 1960. During the Cold War it would become a great asset to temper Russian aggression. It gave twenty-eight years' service to the RAF.

In 1969, English Electric was taken over by GEC, who continued to use the West Works on Strand Road for the production of locomotive traction units, while the East Works still came under the wing of the British Aircraft Corporation, created in 1960, when the government encouraged the merger of several aircraft companies. The first British prototype of the Tornado made its maiden flight from the BAC airfield at Warton in 1974, and the following year a joint venture with the French led to the Jaguar strike aircraft, which had test landings on the newly built M55 before it opened. The Jaguar would go on to serve with the RAF until April 2007 and was very effective in the Gulf War with the coalition forces. The Tornado would become a crucial weapon for the RAF and it was introduced into combat in the first Gulf War in 1991 and in subsequent conflicts – most recently seeing action in Libya and Syria. In 1977, BAC became part of British Aerospace and four years later, in February 1981, the company returned to private ownership as the government sold off their majority shareholding.

These days the Euro-fighter Typhoon built in collaboration with Germany, Italy and Spain is the RAF Quick Reaction Aircraft and is very much on the RAF front line, with both Salmlesbury and Warton being heavily involved in production and assembly. The Typhoon, first flown in 1994, has been successfully employed in conflicts in Libya, Syria and Iraq. The F-35 Lightening is the latest generation of stealth jets and the aircraft, partly built by Lancashire workers, will go into service with the RAF and the Royal Navy.

Nowadays known as BAE Systems, the company, who merged with Marconi Electronic Systems in 1999, abandoned their Strand Road East Works in 1993, but still operate out of town at Salmlesbury and Warton.

Like most vehicle manufacturers, Leyland Motors was involved in manufacturing military equipment during the Second World War, producing Cromwell tanks from 1943 as well as military trucks such as the Leyland Retriever and the Leyland Hippo, which was first manufactured in 1929 and had been developed specially for military purposes. The Centurion tank was developed during the Second World War but not introduced until later, serving the British Army and numerous others for over sixty years. It was a familiar site in such conflicts as the Korean War, the Vietnam War and the Gulf War.

In the aftermath of the Second World War the Ministry of Supply sought fit to have a tank factory built at Farington, which was officially opened in October 1953 having cost £10 million. The spectacular event saw Centurion tanks on display along with others, including a Matilda, Crusader, Cromwell, a famous Comet, a tank that had led the advance into Germany, and a 1917 Mark V tank that was still in running order.

By July 1956 the government decided that the volume of armaments required did not justify the retention of the Farington works and it was bought by Leyland Motors who, in December 1957, named it the Spurrier Works in memory of the late Henry Spurrier, a transport pioneer and founder of the company. With business booming in the heavy commercial vehicle market, and with a workforce of 11,000 in the Leyland and Chorley area alone, the factory would be used to expand their vehicle production as tank orders were completed.

Nonetheless, tank production remained part of their business and by 1976 when the company was Leyland Truck & Bus (incorporated in British Leyland with factories also in Coventry) the biggest ever deal with Iran was clinched. Having already supplied the Iranian government with over 660 Chieftain tanks, an order for 1,200 more was signed.

Preston's affection for tanks was on display in January 1918 when a tank named *Egbert*, in the grey half-light of a winter morning, waddled up Fishergate, waltzed round the corner of Cheapside and settled on the Market Square. A dense crowd gathered to see *Egbert*, who had trundled and clanked up the street on his caterpillar treads with its guns peeping from the barbette. There were scars, mud and rust, along with a gaping hole in its chest where a German gun had put him out of action at Cambrai in France in 1917, all reminders of the battles *Egbert* had fought. The Preston War Savings Committee had arranged with the War Office for the loan of a genuine war tank to visit the town for a week.

Besides the streamers and bunting on display to mark *Egbert*'s arrival, there was a huge barometer that would display the amount of money invested in the Victory war bonds. Within an hour the barometer rose to £350,000, with the borough treasurer investing £45,000 on behalf of the Preston Corporation and the cotton firm of Horrockses pledging £50,000. Astonishingly, by the end of the week over £1 million had been invested, with much of it coming from ordinary folk who had raided their bank accounts or their piggy banks to support the cause.

Egbert – official name Royal Army Tank No. 145 – continued his tour of the Lancashire towns and cities, and the cash poured in from the county's patriotic people. He was finally pensioned off, then presented to Preston in 1919. He had captured Preston's imagination and become a star attraction in Haslam Park. Eventually, in March 1933, *Egbert*, the rusty war veteran, was broken up for scrap iron.

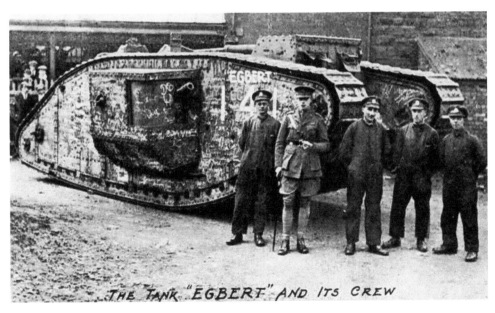

Egbert, the much-loved tank, a veteran of the First World War.

17. Threat from the Sky Above

Quite naturally, Second World War censorship suppressed many an interesting event and only after the conflict did details emerge. Headlines such as 'Raiders Do Little Damage in North West' in the *Lancashire Daily Post* in late August 1940 were commonplace and the report was sketchy in its content. The report described how the first bombs of the war to fall on a North West town had caused little harm, with many inhabitants sleeping through the raid.

In later years, a local resident named Frank Crook, who at the time of the raid lived in Walton-Le-Dale and kept a small holding at Fishwick Bottoms, told how the German planes used to make diversionary raids over the North West whenever they found the flak too hot blitzing Liverpool or Manchester. On that particular August night an enemy aircraft flew over his smallholding, releasing its four bombs that fell into the soft earth. Only one exploded; it left a 3-foot-deep crater. However, the blast was so powerful it blew out the windows of several houses in the Fishwick and London Road areas. The crater was examined by military experts, but he never saw them dig out the unexploded bombs as he worked away on his smallholding in the days that followed.

Other bomb damage included a direct hit by two incendiary bombs at the Park School, Moor Park, in September 1940 – one dropped through the annexe roof and the other into the gymnasium. A more damaging bomb from the same salvo made a direct hit on the army petrol dump in the middle of Moor Park, leaving flames from the inferno to light up the area for a couple of hours until they were quelled. That same night a highly explosive bomb was dropped in-between two semi-detached houses on Longridge Road, near the stone cross memorial. It left a 15-foot-deep crater and severely damaged both houses. Fortunately, the only casualty was one of the dwelling's occupants; he had a cut wrist, having been cleaning his teeth in the bathroom when the explosion took place.

With a number of Lancashire towns playing their part in wartime manufacturing, there was always a threat from German bombers. Leyland Motors, who produced 9,000 trucks, over 3,000 tanks and numerous engines and aircraft components during the war years, had their Lostock Hall plant targeted in late October 1940. A daylight raid saw a lone German plane in the sky above. Fire from the defensive gunners chased the plane off its initial target, but three bombs were dropped over the village. The bombs rained down on terraced streets, killing twenty-five people and injuring many more. Children and a family of eight were among those killed in the Ward Street area of Lostock Hall. On Remembrance Day 1990, to mark the 50th anniversary of the attack, a memorial plaque was unveiled on Ward Street with the names of the twenty-five victims inscribed – Marian Coates (aged seven), Jonathan Clarkson (aged seventy-four) and the entire Watson family were among those indiscriminately killed.

Also coming under enemy fire that night was the Pleasant Retreat Inn, where a memorial was later erected to townspeople who had lost their lives during the war. Also that month the Germans bombed the Farington site of Leyland Motors, killing three people and injuring others. Fortunately, soldiers managed to defuse another unexploded bomb that landed on the roof of the tool room of the factory.

Older residents of Gregson Lane, Brindle, often recall Christmas Day in 1944 when a highly explosive V-2 buzz bomb made an early morning call. The winged bombs were equipped with engines and carried by German planes that released the missiles from the North Sea. This terror from the sky circled Leyland before diving into a field in Gregson Lane. It severely damaged a couple of stone cottages, blew off the roofs of some farm buildings and shattered hundreds of windows, although the only casualties were the occupants of a poultry cabin.

Raiders Do Little Damage in North-West

BY "POST" REPRESENTATIVES

RAIDERS were heard overhead intermittently for a considerable time in the North-West last night.

A heavy barrage of anti-aircraft fire apparently caused some of the enemy to release their bombs from a great height.

There were no casualties and reports indicate that damage was slight, although in one town a house and a works suffered damage.

Near a coastal town bombs were heard to drop not far from a road.

In one town, where bombs were dropped for the first time since the war began, some of the inhabitants slept through the raid and were astonished to hear when they went to work this morning that German aircraft had been active near their homes during the night.

FLASH, LIKE LIGHTNING

The first bombs of the war to fall in one North-West town caused two craters in a market garden and in an adjoining field, dislodged a few panes of glass in a large greenhouse near, broke windows in seven houses at the top of a high bank, removed a chimney pot, injured no one—and

A Nazi 'plane is believed to have been brought down in a South-East area. It was caught in a maze of searchlight beams, from which it could not escape.

A fighter, aided by the beams, could be seen giving chase in and out of the clouds. The enemy could not shake him off.

The beams were extinguished as the planes approached the coast, and the raider was left to the mercy of the fighter who evidently got his target as he returned in a very short time to meet another raider also making a dash for home.

This be greeted with a burst of machine-gun fire which could be plainly heard for some distance over the sea.

In one South-East town, a fire bomb fell close to a hospital. Gas and water mains were also damaged, but repair work was quickly put in hand.

The headlines often hid the truth as German raids increased.

Ward Street in Lostock Hall was blitzed by German bombers.

The memorial plaque on Ward Street unveiled fifty years later.

18. Preston Railway Station Memories

If your train should be delayed you might wish to wander into the Preston railway station waiting room, where you may buy a cup of tea or coffee. While there you cannot fail to be reminded of the Preston Station Buffet, which served the nation so well during the two world wars.

Many local folk had fond memories of the work they did in the buffet, including Kay Davenport, a popular Lancashire author, who in a *Lancashire Life* magazine of the 1960s had this to say about her Second World War experiences:

In 1940 girls who were not called up were expected to do voluntary work, so some of us helped at the buffet which was always open. We thought nothing of walking home in the blackout in the early hours. Some of us also helped at the Fire Station on the telephones, we had learned first aid there, and were told we should always have scissors and string in our pockets in case we met a lady in labour, how we prayed we would never meet one on our way home. We also learned how to slide down a brass pole, a skill I have nor required since!

The huge troop trains, so long you couldn't see both ends when they pulled into the station, were jam packed with soldiers, or sailors or airmen. And we had to dash out with the heavy buckets of hot tea and baskets of sandwiches and buns. The platforms would be a mass of servicemen, some hurrying off on leave, others glad to get off the train for a moment or two. All was noise, the lighting was dim, if an air raid warning sounded there was an eeriness about it all, and a little fear too.

The food was all free, and if the men had to stay on the train, we handed in mugs of tea, just asking that they would leave the empty one's in the carriages. How surprised they were to be greeted by us and all our welcome offerings. The ones who were perhaps going on leave would be laden with kit-bags and rifles, and one night a hefty private cannoned into me as I staggered along with my enamel bucket of scalding hot tea. I went down showered by tea, my thin frock and overall were drenched and my legs were burning. I was picked up and dumped on a kit bag and was soon the centre of attention as the sergeant ordered that some butter be brought from the train. Perhaps they were all from the catering corps. In any event the block of butter was produced and my poor legs soothed, the soldiers producing quite a few wolf-whistles too.

I was soon back at the counter, cutting and covering with margarine hundreds of slices of bread, and filling them with spam or cheeses. Tradespeople from the town donated lots of food. In the evening they would often come along with boxes of apples or other gifts for the servicemen.

There was even a
bed for the night
for some soldiers in
the Preston station
waiting room
in 1915.

As popular as ever
during the Second
World War.

Tea cups and mugs
to be returned.

The Second World War buffet had been officially opened in mid-December 1939. It was reckoned that 1,500 loaves, 1,400 tea cakes, 1,000 potato pies, 500 sausage rolls and over 7,000 cakes were devoured each week by the grateful troops, along with mugs of tea and coffee galore. The buffet never closed its door, with volunteers working day and night until peace reigned in December 1945. It was reported that 12 million cups of tea or coffee had been served and 1,800 local women had volunteered their service during those six years. There was a final plea for the return of mugs, inscribed 'Please return to Preston Station', that had ended up around the world.

This great tradition of serving the troops had begun in August 1915 when the Sailors and Soldiers Free Buffet was officially launched with volunteer staff and paid for by generous donations and fundraising efforts. Those busy, bustling days and nights on Preston railway station are perhaps best summed up by the report on the second anniversary that showed over 1.3 million troops had been served, and all on a budget of £5,074, supplemented by the generosity of local traders who had supplied food willingly at no cost. Among the buffet visitors was Colonel Cooper, who had returned from the war zone. He told the ladies that they were the talk of the trenches on the Western Front for their wonderful hospitality.

The buffet was closed at the end of May 1919 and a correspondent to the *Lancashire Daily Post* commented, 'I have stood on the platform and seen trains arrive full of soldiers and sailors, who were tired and hungry, and have seen their faces light up when they saw the tea and buns handed to them by the ministering angels.'

Consequently, the Preston Station Buffet is not far from the mind when our military heritage is mentioned. Certainly many a member of the armed forces could recall with fondness their brief encounter on Preston railway station where a 'cup of char and a butty' helped them on their way. Their deeds are part of our military heritage and there are poignant reminders of their work within the waiting room to this day.

The Preston railway station waiting room recalls the days of the free buffet for those serving with the armed forces.

19. Home for Soldiers Galore – Fulwood Barracks

Preston has been an important military centre down the centuries, with Fulwood Barracks the base for many soldiers as they prepared to take part in conflicts around the globe. However, it was due to concerns at home that the Fulwood Barracks was actually built. The advent of Charterism in 1838, a political movement that called for parliamentary reforms and a voting system favourable to the working man, left the authorities determined to have the military on hand to quell any disturbances. Subsequently, as riotous behaviour increased among Lancashire folk, the construction of Fulwood Barracks was authorised. The location was seen as ideal to enable troops to be quickly moved to any Lancashire trouble spot on the rapidly expanding rail network.

The preparatory work for the Fulwood Barracks commenced in July 1842. The land occupied by the barracks, barrack yards and enclosed grounds was over 28 acres. The site on which they were erected was once a royal forest and included a portion of the old racecourse, around a mile and a quarter from the town. The contractors for the erection were Messrs Bellhouse of Manchester. The stone used in all the buildings was obtained from the delph at Longridge, taking advantage of the Preston–Longridge railway for transportation. The whole thing was completed in June 1848 and the cost of the works was £137,000. It was reckoned that over 350 builders laboured for over five years to bring the project to completion.

Internally, the buildings were arranged around two large parade grounds – one for the infantry and one for the cavalry. The officers had their own private apartments and the soldiers were housed in dormitories. There were guard houses, officers' quarters, stables, barns, hospitals and even prison cells to cater for military needs.

In truth, the feared Chartist troubles never really developed significantly and the employment of the military force was rarely required. The momentum of Chartism declined as increased prosperity began to take hold in Britain and the Industrial Revolution gathered pace.

It meant, of course, that many battle-ready battalions capable of engaging in conflicts abroad had an ideal base from which to prepare for war. Early arrivals at Fulwood Barracks were the battalions of the 60th Rifles and the 81st Regiment (later the 2nd Loyals), followed by the 52nd Light Infantry and the 89th Infantry. Much to the delight of local folk, the bands of these latter regiments performed fortnightly on the Avenham Walk and were watched by crowds of admirers. It is true to say that those soldiers billeted at the barracks became an integral part of Preston life, although at times their drunken and rowdy behaviour did upset the locals and many a soldier was disciplined for his unbefitting behaviour.

In 1873, Fulwood Barracks became the 12th Brigade Depot, training recruits for the 47th (Lancashire Regiment) and the 81st Loyal Lincoln Volunteers, to whom the Preston-based

Fulwood Barracks was completed in 1848.

On parade in those early days.

The 81st Foot based at Fulwood were encamped at Everton in 1848 to deter Chartist rioters.

Never short of music – the buglers on parade.

3rd Royal Lancashire Militia and the Lancashire Rifle Volunteers were linked. In July 1881, reorganisation of regiments led to the 47th & 81st Regiments becoming the 1st and 2nd Battalions of the Loyal North Lancashire Regiment.

In April 1890, the 5th Dragoon Guards became the first cavalry regiment to make the barracks their HQ, and the newly arrived regiment attracted a great crowd as they paraded to church. The regiment, with a glorious list of battle honours, had first been raised in July 1685 by the Earl of Shrewsbury and was known as the 7th Horse. The regiment, using different titles, continued to serve until 1922 when it merged with other regiments after being involved in both the Boer War and the First World War to great effect.

At the outbreak of the Boer War the 1st (regular) and the 3rd (militia) Battalions of the South Lancashire and the 3rd (militia) Battalion of the Loyal North Lancashire were mobilised at Fulwood, together with the Regular Reservists for the East Lancashires and Loyal North Lancashires, along with active service companies from the volunteer battalions of the East Lancashire and the Loyal North Lancashire's regiments.

Throughout the First World War (1914–18) the depots at Fulwood Barracks received, clothed and equipped many thousands of Regular Reservists and recruits for the East Lancashire and Loyal North Lancashire Regiments, dispatching the latter in drafts to the 3rd (Special Reserve) Battalions of those regiments at Plymouth and Felixstowe respectively, for training before being sent to regular or service battalions abroad.

On the outbreak of the Second World War (1939–1945) the depot of the East Lancashires moved out to form the Infantry Training Centre at Squire's Gate, Blackpool. The Loyals remained at the Infantry Centre at Fulwood Barracks until 1943, the barracks then being occupied by various units with a small Loyals presence.

From 1946 the Fulwood Barracks was used primarily as a training centre, but following the introduction of the National Service Act of 1948 the depots of the East Lancashire and the Loyal Regiment were opened, and over the next decade many thousands of regular and National Service recruits were trained within.

Further reorganisation in 1959 closed the individual regimental depots and centralised the training of recruits. Consequently, the King's Own Royal Border Regiment, the King's Regiment, the Lancashire Regiment (Prince of Wales Volunteers) and the Loyal North Regiment (North Lancashire) all carried out training at Fulwood Barracks until 1971. Adult recruit training was then transferred to Yorkshire and the departure of the Junior Infantryman's Wing followed in 1974, ending over a century of recruit training at the Fulwood Barracks.

From those early days, generations of soldiers have gathered at Preston prior to involvement in military conflicts worldwide. The name of the Loyal North Lancashire Regiment is writ large in the barracks history and acts of bravery and gallantry have been commonplace. Of course regiments have amalgamated and changed names down the years, but their collective identity and history is not forgotten.

In late June 1998, to mark the 150th anniversary of the opening of the Fulwood Barracks, the gates were thrown open to welcome the public to a spectacular military event that included a display of modern high-tech military vehicles, hot-air balloon rides, a freefall parachuting exhibition and a flyover by the Royal Air Force. Later in the day the

Fulwood Barracks soldier athletes with their trophies in 1931.

Return of the Loyals colours in 1945.

The modern-day entrance to Fulwood Barracks on Watling Street Road was home to soldiers from 1848.

The Kimberley Barracks on Deepdale Road, the battalion HQ of the Duke of Lancaster's Regiment.

The soldiers from Kimberley Barracks meet the public often.

annual Beating of the Retreat ceremony took place on the barracks square, with rousing performances from military and civilian bands marking the occasion.

As recently as 2006 it was reckoned that over 500 people lived on the site, with blocks for single soldiers and married quarters for families. At present a link with Fulwood's past as an infantry depot continues at the barracks with the Regimental HQ, the Garrison Chapel and the Lancashire Infantry Museum. It was at the barracks in June 2008 that HM Queen Elizabeth II, colonel in chief of the Duke of Lancaster Regiment, presented new colours to all three battalions of the regiment.

In March 2013 it was announced that despite cuts in the defence budget, the army's North West HQ would remain in the city, with up to £10 million being spent on regional developments. With 450 soldiers based in the city they could expect to see 200 more soldiers arriving, including the 3 Medical Regiment.

Unfortunately, a drastic cull of military bases in the UK announced by the Ministry of Defence in November 2016 means that the Fulwood Barracks is set to close by 2020, bringing to an end a link with the old garrison town. Kimberley Barracks, however, will remain as the base for the territorials.

20. Military Treasures
Aplenty – Infantry Museum

If you truly wish to be transported back in time to the conflicts and confrontations that took place around the world then you should visit the Lancashire Infantry Museum housed within the Fulwood Barracks. The museum enables you to explore the fascinating story of the soldiers of Lancashire in both war and peace.

Preston has never been lacking in its displaying of military heritage, and some may well recall the exhibits that were on display in the recently closed Lancashire Museum on Stanley Street. The building in which that museum was housed was the old courthouse, connected to the former House of Correction. The courthouse was operational by 1829 and thus began a period of seventy-five years when the building served as the place for The Preston Quarter Sessions to be held along with the county court proceedings from 1847.

The former County & Regimental Museum on Stanley Street – later the Museum of Lancashire (now closed).

The days of courts and criminals ended in April 1904 when the new Sessions House building opened on Harris Street. It became the home of the Royal Artillery between 1911 and 1958 and later became the centre for motor vehicle taxing and registration.

It was announced in 1983 that those taxation days were over and that plans were afoot to create a showcase museum for the whole of Lancashire with space for the Duke of Lancaster's yeomanry. From mid-1985, displays honouring the likes of the Loyal Regiment, the Queen's Lancashire Regiment and the efforts on the home front delighted visitors. The museum known as the County and Regimental Museum had a large Howitzer gun on display at the front of the building until 1997, when a change of title to the Museum Of Lancashire took place.

In May 1954, the Regimental Museum within the Fulwood Barracks, which had been closed since the war, was reopened by Brigadier G. Williams, colonel of the Loyal Regiment. The museum had been formed in 1929 to trace the history and achievements of what would become the Queen's Lancashire Regiment. The collection included uniforms, guns and swords from campaigns fought all over the world, as well as an archive and library.

It is truly a delight to visit the museum today, where the displays are enthralling in their telling of the tale. Nowadays it is the Duke of Lancaster's Regiment who carry on the tradition of the Lancashire Infantry Museum. You can visit the Waterloo Room, the Somme Room, the Quebec Room, the magnificent Council Chamber and the Garrison Church of St Albans, all of which have treasures and mementoes on display.

You can see the Salamanca Eagle, a Waterloo Drum, a Kimberley Star, a Russian musket taken at Alma, a Sebastopol bell, the dress uniform tunic of a First World War drummer, a German machine gun seized from the enemy in 1917, a drum that saw service at Dunkirk, playing cards issued to Allied troops during the Iraq War, tales of heroic Victoria Cross awards, regimental colours and standards galore, silver drums presented to the regiment, portraits of gallant soldiers and battles fought, and much more besides. The museum is a place in which you can linger long and absorb the hundreds of years of historical heritage of Preston from the garrison town days.

You will also have the chance to view the regimental colours. In common with most British infantry regiments, the Queen's Lancashire Regiment carries two colours per battalion. The Queen's Colour, based on the Union Flag, displays scrolls bearing selected battle honours from the First and Second World Wars. In the centre, embroidered in gold, is the regimental title and the battalion number is beneath a queen's crown. The Queen's Colours are fringed with crimson and gold alternate strands.

The regimental colour has a royal blue field background, as the Queen's Lancashire is a royal regiment. The red rose of Lancashire is in the centre, surrounded by the regimental title and surmounted by a queen's crown. The regimental motto is displayed below on a union wreath of roses, thistles and shamrocks, and in the four corners are the crests of the regimental forebears: the East Lancashire Regiment, a red rose charged with the sphinx and inscribed 'Egypt'; the Lancashire Regiment, a red rose charged with the Prince of Wales feathers; the South Lancashire Regiment, a sphinx superscripted 'Egypt', charged with the Prince of Wales feathers; the Loyal Regiment (North Lancashire), a red rose charged with the royal crest. The regimental colour is encircled with the laurel wreath awarded for Waterloo, on which are embroidered selected battle honours prior to 1914 and a sphinx commemorating the 1801 victory in Egypt. The regimental colour is fringed with blue and gold alternate strands.

Colours have been carried by the regiment since its formation in 1689. They originally had a tactical purpose, as the regiment's rallying point in battle when soldiers fought in close formation. Defence of the colours was of utmost importance and the selected officers and NCOs who formed the colour party occupied a post of the greatest honour and danger. At Waterloo it is recorded that fourteen sergeants and officers were killed or wounded guarding the colours of the 40th, which was shot almost to pieces. The last occasion when the colours were carried in action by the regiment was at the Battle of Ahmad Khel in Afghanistan in 1880, where the 59th fought in traditional close order to

The regimental colours on display.

defeat charging waves of fanatical tribesmen and twenty selected men were detailed to defend the colours.

The regiment is fortunate to have inherited five sets of silver drums. The drums on display in the museum were subscribed for by all ranks of the South Lancashire Regiment in memory of their comrades who fell in the First World War.

The Salamanca Eagle on display – captured from the French in Napoleonic days.

Right: Model soldiers galore – kitted out for duty.

Below: The Garrison Chapel displays the standards.

21. War Memorials and Memories

There is no doubt that Preston and the surrounding places have always been keen to remember those local servicemen and women who died for their country – often in conflicts far from home. Consequently, our military heritage is recalled in the numerous war memorials that exist around our city.

In late May 1925 an unveiling ceremony took place in Preston Cemetery of the Cross of Sacrifice, which was erected by the Imperial War Graves Commission in memory of upwards of 320 sailors, soldiers and airmen of the town who died during the First World War (1914–18) and are buried therein. The cross, draped in the Union Jack, was unveiled by the pulling of a cord by the Mayor of Preston, Alderman John Roland Hodgson, who spoke of the deep devotion of the men whose lives were lost. Around the base of the centre portion is inscribed, 'Their names liveth for ever'. The cross, which is of Darley stone with a bronze sword of justice embedded, stands 14 feet high. It is positioned at the beginning of the first avenue in the cemetery and in full view from the cemetery gates on New Hall Lane. The memorial is identical to those already erected in other towns and cities in the UK and countries such as France, Italy, Palestine and Egypt. The intention was also to ensure similar simple headstones were placed on all graves of the war dead, as those placed on graves abroad.

The harsh reality of war touched all classes of society. Among the victims of the atrocities were a number of orphaned boys who had spent their formative years at the Harris Orphanage in Fulwood. The long-serving governor of the orphanage was Colonel Thomas Riley Jolly, who, having overseen the training and education of hundreds of youngsters, had been particularly proud when so many old boys willingly enlisted for war duty. After the war Colonel Jolly planned a suitable memorial to honour the memory of those killed, and thanks to the fundraising efforts of a committee of old boys and girls his hopes came to fruition. He was a proud man in late October 1924 when he unveiled the soldier monument in the orphanage grounds. The impressive white marble figure in the form of a youthful soldier standing with his firearm reversed on a pedestal of polished granite, with a dedication inscribed in letters of gold, was to be a lasting reminder of those who had fallen.

Colonel Jolly, speaking with visible emotion, explained how when the call came 127 boys had enlisted and, of those, eighteen had made the supreme sacrifice, with a large number of others being wounded and disabled. He said he was proud of them all and their brave deeds that had been recognised with at least seven military medals.

Colonel Jolly, who became governor of the Harris Orphanage when it opened in 1888, died in September 1929, aged eighty, after spending over forty years caring for the town's orphans. Sadly, more names had to be added to the orphanage memorial death toll after the Second World War, with four former orphan boys and a girl giving their lives for the country.

The 'Cross of Sacrifice' in Preston Cemetery.

The war victims of the Harris Orphanage are remembered.

On Meadow Street at the front of St Ignatius RC Church (nowadays the Cathedral of St Alphonsa), stands a war memorial dedicated to the men of that parish who had been killed in the First World War. It was unveiled in late March 1922 by Colonel John Shute, watched by the Rector Father Frederick Parry along with other clergy and members of the armed forces as a large crowd gathered. The memorial, built of Portland stone, stands over 22 feet high and is mounted upon a moulded plinth. A crucifix stands aloft with the figures of a sailor and soldier on either side. On the bronze plaques surrounding the memorial are the names of the 228 men of the parish who gave their lives in the conflict. It was paid for by subscriptions from the parishioners.

In mid-March 1921 a memorial to the men of Penwortham who fell or served during the First World War was unveiled by Major-General T. H. Shoubridge. A procession of relatives and friends of the fallen men walked through Penwortham to the Liverpool Road site headed by the Preston Discharged Sailors and Soldiers Band. The war memorial, takes the form of a granite rustic cross, was erected by public subscription. The names of the fallen are inscribed on a stone tablet, while in a recess was placed a parchment record of all who had served in the war. In all, 144 names were recalled, with seventy-two of those having died in the conflict.

In the very centre of Lostock Hall you cannot fail to be impressed by the war memorial that now stands on Hope Terrace. It was unveiled in mid-December 1924 by Colonel C. J. Trimble, who spoke of the gallantry and self-sacrifice of the victims. Nowadays it commemorates the lives of eighty-three local servicemen lost in both world wars. The memorial depicts the figure of Peace mounted on a pedestal of granite and stands over 15 feet tall.

Just around the corner on Brownedge Road is another striking war memorial, which was rescued from its old Lostock Hall Methodist Church site. It contains the names of seventy-nine people who were involved in the First World War conflict. Of those, eleven men were killed, sixty-six returned from battles, and it also includes the names of two nurses, Jesse True and Ethel Calleley, who nursed the stricken.

In the South Ribble area, if you visit the roundabout at the end of Watkin Lane at the entrance to the newly created St Catherine's Park, you will see a 40-foot-tall monument to the fallen soldiers of South Ribble. It depicts the silhouette of a First World War soldier, a symbolic poppy and the conflict dates. The names of 682 fallen soldiers are embossed in steel on the rear of the memorial and on a plaque on the trench structure within the peace garden.

In 1921, on the November anniversary of the Armistice the unveiling of a wayside Celtic cross was carried out by Lieutenant-Colonel W. Bowes in memory of the nine men of the village of Broughton who gave their lives in the First World War. The war memorial stands 16 feet tall and is constructed from Longridge stone, executed by M. Kay of Longridge. The names of the fallen are engraved on the plinth, surrounded by a pavement with steps leading from the roadway. It had cost over £300 and was paid for by the fundraising activities of the villagers who recognised the self-sacrifice made by their fallen men.

Within the grounds of County Hall in Preston, off Fishergate Hill, where Christ Church once flourished, there is a war memorial cross of grey Cornish granite. It stands 12 feet tall in the old graveyard of the church and was unveiled in July 1921 by Revd T. A. Schonberg, who stated it was a moment of proud remembrance of the sixty-nine men connected with the church who had given their lives in the First World War. The memorial had cost £280 to erect and had been possible through the parishioners' relentless pursuit of subscriptions. Like so many others, the memorial cross at Christ Church had another brass plaque added after 1945, recording yet more victims from the Second World War.

Should you visit the neglected graveyard of St Paul's Church (now the home of Rock FM) you will see a memorial cross in one corner erected by the parishioners of St Paul's in honour of the 125 men of the parish killed during the First World War. It was unveiled at the end of August 1920 by Lieutenant-Colonel S. Simpson, who read out the names of each of the men. He then told the large crowd gathered around the monument that some of those killed were personally known to him. Having journeyed to France with them he was all too aware that they had fought magnificently and had showed great devotion to duty.

On the same evening Emmanuel Church was packed as parishioners paid tribute to their war victims. Two memorial windows were unveiled in the baptistery and Revd W. D. Richards quoted the biblical text, 'Greater love hath no man than this, that a man lay down his life for his friend.'

A month later a large crowd gathered outside the Church of St Mary Magdalene on Ribbleton Avenue to witness the unveiling of a war memorial to honour the eighteen men of that parish who had been killed during the First World War. The monument is in

The war memorial outside St Ignatius Church on Meadow Street.

The Penwortham War Memorial, unveiled in 1921.

The South Ribble War Memorial – a modern tribute to the fallen.

At the centre of Lostock Hall is a 'Peace' tribute to the fallen.

the shape of a stone cross made of light Boltonwood stone, stands over 12 feet high and sits on a 5-foot-square base with three steps at the front. A stone laurel wreath hangs over the cross, and a sword runs parallel with the face of the column. Three bronze panels record the names of the fallen with an inscription. The memorial, funded by parishioners, cost £200.

One of the earliest to display their grief were the members of the St Matthews Church congregation who, in December 1919 before a crowd of 1,000, unveiled a memorial window to the fallen soldiers and sailors from the church and school. The vicar, Revd C. Townson, reminded those gathered that nearly 700 men of St Matthews had answered the call and that ninety-nine of them had perished performing their duty. The two light window depicts the archangels Michael and Gabriel, holding the scroll of honour inscribed with their names.

To observe the memorial to the war dead of the parish of St Wilfrid's RC Church and the closely connected Preston Catholic College, you must make a visit inside the church. Positioned on the right-hand side amid the Station of the Cross is a large marble crucifix set on an altar and flanked by two tablets that record the names of 114 men killed during the war. This includes some forty-eight who were former pupils of the Jesuit-run Catholic College. The memorial was unveiled by Father Kopp on the middle Sunday of April 1922. On the sanctuary floor nowadays are two more tablets commemorating the dead from the church and the college during the Second World War.

A service of dedication and the unveiling of a war memorial took place at St Mary's (Church of England) in Preston in the first week of August 1922. Within the (now closed) church a memorial plaque contains the names of the eighty men who lost their lives in the First World War. Six of them died in the UK and are buried in Preston Cemetery, with the others laid to rest in foreign fields. An exhibition was held within the Lancashire Museum on Stanley Street prior to its closure that told of the fate of many.

It is doubtful that a larger crowd had ever gathered in the Preston Market Square than the one that assembled in mid-June 1926 to witness the unveiling of the Preston War Memorial. A dense crowd of people even filled the adjoining streets. In the centre of the square the military gathered and the memorial was lined with ex-servicemen and women. The man chosen to perform the ceremony was the distinguished Admiral of the Fleet, Earl Jellico, who pulled the cord that saw the Union Jack fall away to uncover the sculptured figure of Victory. In his speech he remarked that it was a great honour to take part in a ceremony in recognition of the almost 2,000 men of Preston who had given their lives for king and country during the First World War.

The cenotaph was built to the design of Sir Giles Gilbert Scott, grandson of Sir George Gilbert Scott, the man who had designed the Preston Town Hall in Victorian days. The sculptor who toiled long to create the 70-foot-tall monument was Henry Alfred Pegram. The cenotaph carved from Portland stone has a square, slightly tapered column and at the front is the tableaux that depicts grieving Victory in armour holding aloft two laurel crowns, surrounded by representations of the dead. At the very top of the monument there is a sculptured empty tomb with cherubs and strands of foliage carved around it. The names of the servicemen honoured are inscribed on marble tablets within the Harris Museum; the roll of honour is on permanent display on the ground floor.

As recently as 2013 the cenotaph was fully modernised and extended and now includes carvings in recognition of those who lost their lives in the Second World War and subsequent conflicts. The cenotaph is regarded as an exceptional Grade I listed war memorial. It is fitting that wherever you wander in Preston you are likely to come across a memorial that recalls the brave deeds of those lost in battle.

The memorial inside St Wilfrid's Church is dedicated to the men of the parish and the old boys of Preston Catholic College who gave their lives.

Paying tribute to Preston's fallen in 1926.

22. Remembrance – Part of Our Heritage

It was fitting in November 2018 that a great crowd gathered around Preston Cenotaph and fell silent to mark 100 years since the end of the First World War. That conflict and all those wars before and after are part of the military heritage of our city.

As part of the anniversary of the Armistice a number of silhouettes of the once familiar 'Tommy' soldiers have appeared around Lancashire; a couple stood either side of the cenotaph to mark the centenary. The Preston railway station, a roundabout on Eastway and the new Preston Market Hall were also the setting for those lone figures during the year.

Among those on parade at the Remembrance Day gathering of 2018 were the Preston branch of the Royal British Legion. This organisation, founded back in July 1921 by Field Marshall Earl Haig, brought together many of the associations of ex-servicemen and women of all ranks. From its very beginnings, Preston embraced the new initiative and that year they established a club room in Bamber's Yard, Preston from where they had concerts and fundraising events.

Such was the success of the British Legion that by 1931 there were 3,635 branches throughout the UK, a third of them having a thriving women's section. By then, their 'Poppy Factory' in Richmond was employing over 270 severely disabled men.

The work of the British Legion was felt in all quarters of society. An example of the Preston branch assistance came in September 1932 when it was announced that over 300 war medals had been sold to a Fishergate bullion dealer. Believing the medals had probably been sold during difficult times by ex-servicemen who were struggling for employment, the Preston branch immediately got in contact with the dealer and persuaded him to sell the medals to them, following which the organisation set about the task of tracing the original owners and reuniting the medals with the heroes who had earned them.

By February 1939 a new Preston branch HQ was opened in Grimshaw Street, with local members numbering over 600. During the previous year the benevolent committee had sanctioned payments of over £1,000 to local Legion members and their dependants. Although there was only £64 left in the charity kitty, the Preston branch were confident about their future.

To the credit of what is now the Royal British Legion, they were on hand to assist and guide those who fought in the Second World War and future conflicts worldwide. The veterans of the organisation are often involved in civic and military events, proudly displaying their medals and parading the colours.

The Remembrance Day ceremony was an opportunity for all the civic and military organisations connected with the city to march to the cenotaph to pay their respects. Among them were the 4th Battalion of the Duke of Lancaster Regiment; the regular soldiers of the 5 Medical Support Royal Army Medical Corps, who are stationed at Fulwood Barracks; and the Lancashire Army Cadet Force, who are cap badged to the Duke

Members of the Royal British Legion parade with the colours.

Regular soldiers from the 4th Battalion of the Duke of Lancaster Regiment Army Reserve from Kimberley Barracks march to the cenotaph.

Marching in combat dress, the Lancashire Army Cadet Force – cap badged to the Duke of Lancaster's Regiment.

Regular soldiers from 5 Medical Support Royal Army Medical Corps from Fulwood Barracks prepare to parade.

Of Lancaster Regiment. They were joined by sailors of the Royal Navy, members of the Royal Air Force, police officers, firefighters, cadets galore, scouts and guides, with the Brindle Band accompanying them playing their stirring military music.

In late June 2018 the servicemen and women of Preston came together to celebrate Armed Forces Day with the Duke of Lancaster Regiment, participating in a Freedom Parade. Many local organisations gathered on the Market Square, with displays, military equipment, merchandise and charity stalls marking what is now an annual event. The first Armed Forces Day was held in the UK in 2009, replacing the short-lived Veterans Day started in 2006.

The centenary of the Victoria Cross awarded to James Towers and the Victoria Cross awarded to another local hero, Private William Young, for his bravery in December 1915 on the Western Front, were marked in 1918 by the placing of plaques in front of the cenotaph commemorating their achievements.

Preston is also blessed that from time to time the band of the Queen's Lancashire Regiment provides us with military marching music. The band is one of the finest in the British Army and are no stranger to concert halls and showgrounds in the county, with many a parade or occasion of pageantry being enhanced by their appearance.

The military heritage of Preston stretches back down the centuries and the remembrance of the battles fought and the heroic bravery is interwoven in the very fabric of 'Proud Preston'.

Footnote: 'See The Conquering Hero Comes', the story of Private William Henry Young is recorded in *People of Old Preston* by Keith Johnson (1994).

A large crowd gathered for the Remembrance Day service in 2018.

The lone silhouette of a soldier in the new Market Hall, 2018.

Help for Heroes – supporting Preston's Armed Forces veterans in 2018.

The Queen's Lancashire Regimental Band is always welcome in Preston.

About the Author

Keith Johnson is Preston born and bred. His previous works include the bestselling 'Chilling True Tales' series of books featuring Preston, Lancashire and London, and the popular *People of Old Preston, Preston Remembered, Preston Through Time, Preston in the 1960s, Secret Preston, Preston in 50 Buildings, Preston History Tour, Preston at Work, A–Z of Preston* and *Now That's What I Call Preston* books. For over a decade he has contributed numerous feature articles on local history to the *Lancashire Post*, and since 2011 has written a weekly 'Court Archive' for the *LP Retro* magazine.

Keith was educated at St Augustine's Boys' School in Preston prior to attending the Harris College where he gained his qualifications for a career in engineering, spending forty years working for the printing-press manufacturer Goss.

Acknowledgements

I must acknowledge the help given to me by the staff of the Harris Community Library in Preston, who willingly assist as I delve into their archives – their records make my research that much easier. I am also indebted to the Lancashire Infantry Museum, who are an inspiration for all those interested in military history.

My appreciation also goes to the newspaper reporters of the past who, in chronicling the events of their day, made this book possible. *The Lancashire Post, Preston Guardian, Preston Chronicle, Preston Pilot,* and *Preston Herald* all provided me with information from their publications. Likewise, I thank the Preston historians of old, in particular Anthony Hewitson, Peter Whittle, Charles Hardwick, Henry Fishwick and William Pollard, who provided me with valuable sources of information.

Besides my own collection of images and illustrations, I would like to thank the *Lancashire Post* for permission to use images that are nowadays stored in the Preston Digital Archive. Also, my thanks go to Richard H. Parker, the creator of the PDA, for use of images from that source, and to Mike Hill, communities editor of the *Lancashire Post*, who is ever helpful in my research.

My thanks also to Pat Crook for cheerfully checking my manuscript and putting her literary skills at my disposal once again.